TONY GREGORY

ABOUT TONY GREGORY

'Gregory was a unique figure in Irish politics over almost thirty years. We may never see his like again and that is a great loss for the people of Dublin Central, politics, our democratic system and, especially, for those who were closest to him personally and politically.'

Eamon Gilmore in Dáil tribute after Gregory's death

'He possesses an amazingly quick political mind. He is highly articulate. He can express his case with clinical brevity and lethal effect. It is done in a quietly effective manner. He never rambles, and does not like to see others waffling. Time is too important to be wasted.'

Frank Kilfeather, writing about the young Tony Gregory in The Irish Times

'He was a true messenger of the people who served his community with sincerity, commitment and skill.'

Taoiseach Brian Cowen speaking in the Dáil on the death of Tony Gregory

Robbie Gilligan is Professor of Social Work and Social Policy at Trinity College, Dublin. He grew up on Dublin's northside and can trace some of his family roots to the north inner city, to Dominick Street and Bayview Avenue. He also spent most of his schooldays at Belvedere College, located in the inner city. In his last years at school, he was a volunteer in the Belvedere Youth Club, which serves inner city young people. There he first met Fergus McCabe, who was later to be one of Tony Gregory's closest political associates. During his training as a social worker, he spent various stints working in the inner city and later came back to serve there as a health board social worker. He became involved in the establishment of Tabor House and 69 Amiens Street, two residential care centres for local children and young people in the north inner city. He got to know Tony Gregory as the latter was setting out on his political career and was impressed by Tony's serious and practical commitment to social justice. He signed up to help Tony out in the early election campaigns and played a minor part in the Gregory Deal process. With colleagues Philip Curry, Lindsey Garratt and Jenny Scholtz, he has published a study of inter-ethnic relations in inner-city primary schools, 'Where to from here?' (Liffey Press, 2011). Robbie is also Associate Director of the Children's Research Centre at Trinity College and President of Childwatch International Research Network.

TONY GREGORY

ROBBIE GILLIGAN

THE O'BRIEN PRESS
DUBLIN

First published 2011 by The O'Brien Press Ltd,
12 Terenure Road East, Rathgar, Dublin 6, Ireland.
Tel: +353 1 4923333; Fax: +353 1 4922777
E-mail: books@obrien.ie
Website: www.obrien.ie

ISBN: 978-1-84717-226-6

British Library Cataloguing-in-Publication Data
A catalogue record for this title is available from the British Library

1 2 3 4 5 6 7 8 9 10
11 12 13 14 15

Editing, typesetting, layout and design: The O'Brien Press Ltd

Printed and bound by ScandBook AB, Sweden
The paper used in this book is produced using pulp from managed forests

DEDICATION
To Tony Gregory's supporters

ACKNOWLEDGEMENTS

It has been a great privilege and challenge to write this book about Tony Gregory. I am very grateful to the many people who have supported me in the project. Noel Gregory has always been very supportive and exceptionally generous with his time, his memories and his family records. I first came to know Fergus McCabe when I was seventeen or so as a volunteer in the Belvedere Youth Club where we both made our first connection to the north inner city. Fergus has been a friend and inspiration ever since. In this project, he has been most helpful, ever willing to delve into his memory on this detail or that. Many other people were very generous also, with time, recollections, leads and access to material: Mick Rafferty who shared good memories and stories, Maureen O'Sullivan who drew on her political association and personal friendship with Tony over all his political career, Annette Dolan, his partner in the later years, who went to a lot of trouble to help me track down various material. There were many people with strong links to the inner city as natives or 'blow ins', or who had an association with Tony through friendship, political work, or some combination who kindly agreed to answer my questions or be interviewed – Philip Boyd, Christy Burke, Pat Carthy, Liz Doyle, John Farrelly, Pauline Kane, Joe Kelly, Seanie Lambe, John Lynch, Marie Metcalfe, David Norris, Jim Sheridan, Derek Speirs, Valerie Smith and Pádraig Yeates. Many of my colleagues in Trinity College showed interest in the project and offered helpful insights or comment in the course of my work on the book. Professor Michael Gallagher, Department of Political Science, was most generous, as always, in allowing me tap his encyclopaedic knowledge of Irish politics to help me track down or check certain more esoteric information. Other colleagues who offered helpful comments or insights include Professor Eunan O'Halpin, School of Histories and Humanities, and colleagues in my own school, the School of Social Work and Social Policy: Dr Shane Butler, Dr Barry Cullen, Dr Philip Curry, Maeve Foreman, Gloria Kirwan and Dr Eoin O'Sullivan.

I am most grateful to the Dublin City Archive who helped me in various ways. I owe a great debt of gratitude to Ide Ní Laoghaire and Michael O'Brien whose good advice and faith in the project were very important.

Most of all, I must thank my wife Mary Quinn, and our three daughters, Aoife, Sinead and Orla, for their patience and support throughout a project that ate up huge amounts of spare time in an already busy life.

I thank everybody who helped me with the researching and the writing of the book. They have helped make it a better work. Any remaining errors are, of course, my own responsibility.

Robbie Gilligan 2011

CONTENTS

PART I

. . . . . .

FROM THE

CRADLE TO

THE DEAL

. . . .

CHAPTER 1

· · · · · ·

Tony's Early Life

I believe her spirit is still somewhere out there, as I know that she totally loved me. I have some sort of feeling that the intense love for your children doesn't die – it doesn't go away.

Tony Gregory[1]

Tony's mother, Ellen Judge, was born in 1904, the eldest of four children. The family lived on a small farm in Croghan, County Offaly, on the edge of the Bog of Allen, a large peat bog near the Electricity Supply Board's turf-fired Rhode power station. Ellen went to Dublin when she was sixteen in the late 1920s and worked as a waitress in Jury's Hotel, then situated in Dame Street. She lived in a flat on Amiens Street. Tony often said that she had hoped to be a teacher, but had been prevented in this ambition by financial pressures in her family as she grew up.[2] She and Anthony Gregory married relatively late in life, having met through a relative of the Gregorys who had an Offaly connection. They had two children, Noel born in 1945 and Anthony (Tony) in 1947.

Ellen had a very strong work ethic and she was ambitious for her children and for the family. This was a time when few women worked outside the home, yet, even after her children were born, Ellen worked on a casual basis as a waitress in the highly regarded Paradiso restaurant. She did this to supplement the family income and to help save for the family home.

The couple had bought a house, having been refused a place on the Dublin Corporation housing waiting list because they didn't have enough children. The family had lived for twelve years in a one-roomed flat on Charleville Avenue, Ballybough, in a house belonging to a relative, but Ellen had set her sights on a flat in the new Corporation flats complex – Jim Larkin House – then being built on the North Strand near the Five Lamps. But when she went to the Dublin Corporation housing office to apply, the official said, 'Come back when you have six', as he glanced at her two children. When Ellen told him she was too old to have more children, he simply shrugged his shoulders. From that incident can be traced the deep motivation that drove Tony throughout his political career – he referred to it many times in media interviews. The sense of outrage he felt on behalf of his mother, and others in the same boat, was palpable. The Gregory family's experience was not unusual.

The 1950s were very hard times economically in Ireland. Emigration was rampant – people had lost hope in the future of the country and were forced to try their luck in the cities of Britain and beyond. The economic and political realities of the time meant that there was not enough money allocated by the State to house building to match the demand from local authority housing lists. But the high levels of emigration and economic decline also meant that house prices ultimately fell severely, allowing some working-class families actually to contemplate buying their own home. Tony's parents responded to the Council's rebuff by saving about £700, a lot of money in those days, to buy a house in Sackville Gardens, a small, quiet cul-de-sac bordering the Royal Canal at Ballybough, very close to Croke Park, where the family lived from then on.

Thus both Tony's parents worked and struggled to earn enough to pay for their family home. Tony would live in that house most of his life and was eventually buried from there. Ellen was clearly a determined woman and did what had to be done to make things work – neighbours recall seeing her climbing up on the roof of the house to fix some problem, not an everyday activity for women in those times. Ellen was also independent minded, a woman who had her own opinions and stood her ground, though Noel recalls her being very reticent about her politics and never declaring how she voted.

His mother loved animals and instilled this love in Tony. The large back garden of the family home was rich in nature – there were tomatoes in the greenhouse, there were racing pigeons, a favourite hobby of inner city men, and there was a hen run, complete with chickens and a cockerel. Noel also remembers pigs there when they were growing up. Jim Sheridan, Tony's long-time friend, grew up in the same area but now lives in the country in Westmeath. He says that having pets as youngsters was formative for both Tony and himself in developing a lifelong love of animals and a deep enjoyment of animals in their more natural habitats.[3] Tony also spent many summer holidays with his mother's people on the family farm in Offaly and this gave him a strong connection to the countryside. He recalled packing his clothes into a cardboard box and heading to Busáras, the central bus station serving destinations outside Dublin. With the box loaded onto the top of the single-decker bus, he would set off for the country.[4] His enjoyment of the outdoors was also nurtured, no doubt, by time spent in the scouts. The scouts would have provided diversion and fun, but also important outings beyond the city – camping trips and the like, precious for boys living in the grim confines of the 1950s inner city.

By comparison with his mother, Tony's father, Anthony, was a dyed-in-the-wool city man, who featured less prominently in his son's public recollections of childhood. Anthony was the seventh-born, and the youngest boy in a family of eight. The 1911 Census records Anthony's family living at 162 North Strand, the ten of them sharing three rooms in a section of that house.

Both Anthony, and earlier his father, Robert, had lived through momentous times. Robert – Tony and Noel's grandfather – was an Englishman from Devon and a Protestant by birth, but his love of his wife-to-be, Esther, had brought him to live in Dublin and led him to convert to Catholicism. He was a tailor, with much of his business coming from the provision of uniforms for the British Army, which, of course, had a large garrison in the city in the days before political independence was achieved in 1922. Coincidentally, Robert once helped to save the lives of two Royal Irish Constabulary (RIC) policemen at his front door on the North Strand. They were being attacked by a crowd in disturbances linked to the 1913 Lock-out when, in an attempt to break a strike, major employers in the city had called a lockout of workers to intimidate the strikers into submission – the employers were fearful of the threat that organised labour could represent. There had been baton charges in O'Connell Street by the RIC earlier that day against a public meeting of the strikers, and hundreds had been injured. As the marchers drifted away from O'Connell Street, some of them met up with another group on the North Strand coming back from a union meeting at Croydon Park, and feelings ran high as they all discussed the events in the city centre. Two RIC men in uniform happened to be in the vicinity and proved a ready target for the crowd's anger, until they were rescued by Tony's grandfather.[5]

Tony's father worked as a warehouseman for the Dublin Port and Docks Board. He had previously owned a shoemaker's business under the railway bridge at Ballybough, very close to the North Strand, but it proved too difficult at the time to make a living as a cobbler as economic hardship meant that people could not always afford to come back and pay for shoes they had left in for repair. Like most men relying on the docks for employment, Anthony worked on a casual basis. It could not have been easy to switch from running a business to being dependent on casual work, but he would have had little choice in the hard times of 1950s Ireland. Some work was better than no work. Tony recalled that 'he was unemployed as often as he was working.' Thus Anthony's income was unreliable; some days he got work, other days he didn't – it all depended on the number of boats and the volume of goods passing through the port.

Anthony's politics, however, were obvious to his boys, unlike their mother's. Noel recalls that their father had a photo of Michael Collins cut out from a newspaper pinned over his bed until the day he died. Tony explained that while his father revered Collins, he 'despised' De Valera – such clear and polarised views were common in people of this Civil War generation, Collins and De Valera representing, of course, the opposing pro-Treaty and anti-Treaty sides respectively. In the days before television, the Gregory family, like many, passed the time in storytelling and Tony later said that listening to his father's stories about momentous events that he had lived through, such as the 1913 Lockout and the 1916 Rising, had been hugely powerful in awakening his own political interests and views, even if they did eventually differ from his father's.

One of Tony's father's proudest possessions was a gramophone player. He loved to listen to John McCormack and Enrico Caruso, among other famous singers of the time. Tony remembered summer evenings when his father would push up the sash window of their one-roomed flat in Charleville Avenue, wind up the gramophone player and place it at the window – and the whole street would be treated to a free concert![6] One of Tony's own musical passions as a teenager was Elvis Presley, and his friend, Jim Sheridan, recalls Tony sporting a hairstyle in honour of his hero – typical for boys of his time.

For Tony, home provided many forms of encouragement to learn and to connect with the wider world. Tony and Noel, as boys, were members of the local public library across the canal on Charleville Mall. Tony also became an altar boy and attended the religious services at St Agatha's parish church, again just over the canal. The two brothers joined the Legion of Mary and attended meetings in its then headquarters in nearby North Great George's Street, not much more than a few blocks away. Founded in Dublin in 1921 by Frank Duff, the Legion of Mary was, and still is, a significant international lay Catholic organisation devoted to the religious development of its members and offering assistance to others. Growing up with a religious mother would certainly have influenced Tony's decision at a young age to join the Legion. In his *Hot Press* interview, however, Tony states his position on religion later in his life:

> It's somewhere out there [his mother's love], and, in some sense, is watching over me ... That may be a hangover from what I would call excessive religion in childhood. It may also just be an emotional response to my own love for my mother. I believe that when you love somebody so much, that person never dies, they are out there somewhere forever. I would love to believe she is in heaven. But when I bring that down to logic, I have to say that I just don't have the beliefs that I was brought up to have. I don't see any logic in such belief.

Another friend of Tony's, Pat Carthy, grew up on the opposite side of the Royal Canal. Tony was some years older. For a long time, they just knew each other to see, but Pat then had a rude introduction to Tony when Tony was about fourteen. Tony had an air gun, and one day was taking potshots at suitable targets from his bedroom window. One of these turned out to be an unsuspecting Pat on the other side of the canal. Pat understandably took some exception and told his father, who immediately stormed around to the Gregory front door to remonstrate. Calm was restored and some days later Tony muttered an apology to Pat, saying, 'I didn't think my aim was that good.' They went on to be friends for life. Pat recalls an interesting glimpse into the hard times of the 1950s that Tony and many of his generation experienced. It arose from some amusing late-night competitive banter many years later between Tony and John Kelly, brother of The Dubliners' singer Luke, as they looked back on the extent of their endurance of poverty in their respective childhoods. John could remember his family buying the white cloth sacks in which flour was delivered through the docks – the Kellys lived on Sheriff Street, close to the docks. These sacks would be ripped open and then sewn up to serve as sheets. Tony retorted that his family were not in that league – to be able to afford the sacks. The Gregorys, Tony asserted, knew harder times. They relied on old army coats thrown on the bed to keep them warm. However, Pat reckons that Tony's parents' efforts probably shielded their boys from the worst extremes of poverty, but that Tony would certainly have seen terrible deprivation in his neighbourhood, for example in the cottages which were to give way to the Corporation flats at Croke Villas, close to where both Tony and Pat grew up. Pat thinks these experiences would have had a powerful influence on Tony's early political formation and motivation. (Ultimately Pat himself became a volunteer youth worker, and, in time, he was also to become a keen member of the Gregory political machine, just one example of the kind of person attracted to supporting Tony.)

EDUCATION

Above all else, Tony's mother deeply valued education, a point he stressed on many occasions. Like many country people, she had a passionate belief that education was the escape route from the hardship and hard work that were the lot of her husband.[7] Interestingly, Tony noted that his father was less preoccupied with the importance of education, reflecting perhaps the lower priority it was traditionally accorded in working-class Dublin, or more precisely, perhaps, indicating the lack of any evidence locally that education made a positive difference to life's chances.[8]

Tony recalled that his mother had scoured the local area for the school that would take her children at the youngest age so that her sons could get started as early as possible on the educational ladder. She discovered that a pre-school in Hill Street, run by the Loreto nuns for local, inner-city children, took three-year-olds (the local children came in the back door on

Hill Street to the complex; the front opened onto North Great George's Street, and was a well known school serving the daughters of middle-class Dubliners). Tony talked of being 'petrified' on his first day as he was plucked from his mother's arms by the nun, Mother Alberta. From Hill Street, he moved in time to North William Street primary school, which was run by the French Sisters of Charity, as they were known – the Daughters of Charity to give them their formal title. The school could claim the celebrated Dublin playwright and 'character', Brendan Behan, among its alumni. Tony then went on to 'Canniers' – St Canice's, a Christian Brothers' primary school serving the local population. It was run by the same community of Brothers as ran O'Connell's secondary school on the North Circular Road, which was then a 'posh' Christian Brothers' secondary school that attracted middle-class boys from all over the city.

In Tony's schooldays, primary school (serving children aged roughly from four or five to twelve) was free, as remains the case today, unless parents wanted their child to attend a private, fee-paying school. But secondary school was a different matter in the days before 'free education'. It wasn't until the mid-sixties that the pioneering and colourful Minister for Education, Donogh O'Malley, uncle of the Progressive Democrat founder, Dessie O'Malley, announced the abolition of fees from 1969 for admission to mainstream secondary schools up, thereby establishing 'free education' and achieving one of the greatest social reforms in independent Ireland. But in Tony's schooldays, it was very rare for a child from the inner city of Dublin or any other working-class family to go to secondary school. The fees were simply beyond the reach of their parents. The only chance they had of getting education in (the more academic) secondary school as opposed to a technical school was to win a Corporation or County Council scholarship through a highly competitive examination. These scholarships were very scarce – there was, for example, only one such scholarship for every twenty-four students leaving national school in 1965.[9]

At his mother's prompting, Tony was groomed to sit the exams for the Dublin Corporation scholarship. Even at such a young age (twelve) he was strongly aware that success would lead to a place for him in secondary school, that could also open up a route to college or university, while failure would mean abandoning the idea of further serious study. In the absence of a scholarship, the only alternative for a young person from humble means would be a place in a technical or vocational school (Tech) with a view, at best, to taking up a trade; or to join a religious order, as his brother was to do. Tony recalled how the odds were stacked against the those from the wrong side of the tracks and how he succeeded in getting his scholarship for O'Connell's during his final year in primary school. Tony speaks here of luck, but clearly ability was a big element in his success in the scholarship examination.

Basically, I ended up in the scholarship class and while I was there I was never given any encouragement. Canice's was a local school for local kids and it followed that if you went to Canice's then you went on to a Tech in Parnell Square or wherever. There never was anyone to say: Listen, it might be better for you to go to a secondary school and from there to third level.

However, in the scholarship class there was a chance to get the Dublin Corporation Scholarship which got you into O'Connell's secondary school. I was lucky enough to get one of these.

You'd go into City Hall and there'd be all these tables laid out with glass cabinets on them. In these were lists of names, and the first one hundred and twenty names out of the whole of Dublin would get a scholarship. I got 32nd on the list.

I could never forget going home to tell my mother, who was absolutely delighted. Before that result came out I had done the entrance exam, like everyone else, for Parnell Square Tech and was on my way up there but for this scholarship business.[10]

Prior to the building of the Civic Offices on Wood Quay, City Hall was the formal headquarters of the City Council; now largely decorative and ceremonial in function, it would certainly have been quite an adventure for the boy from Sackville Gardens to make his way across the river on his own and to enter this intimidating world of formality, quite a distance then, socially and even physically, from his world along the Royal Canal.

Thus, early in his education, Tony was exposed to the two-tier nature of an educational system based on the segregation of the social classes. He recalled that there were different expectations for students in O'Connell's too, depending on their social background. The 'scholarship boys' were told repeatedly not to bother with the idea of university, then a much less common option than it is today. Teacher training college was the most they should aspire to, the option they were told to consider. The Christian Brothers themselves had absorbed the message that university was an elite institution set up to serve the social elite, and they were willing to transmit that same message to their charges. The reality, of course, was probably that most of the Brothers themselves had not been to university either, and given their often relatively humble social background, they too did not aspire to university study. The Brothers saw no reason to challenge this social order; they were loyal to a social group from which they themselves were excluded, by social norms or their own expectations. The Brothers were, in effect, both the victims and guardians of what was effectively a form of social apartheid, though these social divisions may have come at a very high emotional price for both the Brothers and the boys in their charge.

While Tony went on to win the scholarship to O'Connell's, Noel, on the other hand, remembers well how he had incurred his mother's wrath for not winning a place in O'Connell's secondary school; instead he had stayed on to seventh class at St Canice's, and then joined the Christian Brothers at thirteen years of age – the way things were done then. He remembers the day a Brother called to his house to drive him and another boy to the

Christian Brothers' preparatory college in Baldoyle. Looking back, Noel thinks the Christian Brothers instilled in both himself and Tony a love of history and politics, and of learning – or, at the very least, it might be said that they reinforced the message the boys had been given at home. On leaving school, Noel stayed in the Christian Brothers and eventually took a Bachelor in Arts degree by night at University College Dublin (UCD). Through her boys, their mother could enjoy the educational achievement that had eluded her.

Spruced up and full of his mother's expectations, the scholarship boy, Tony, carried his school bag over the threshold into O'Connell's secondary school for the first time in September 1960. As he settled down at his new desk, he was hardly to know that his next six years in the school would coincide with a period of remarkable change and ferment both in Ireland and abroad. Most of the parents of the boys joining that first-year class cannot have held great hopes for their sons' futures in Ireland. A general pessimism filled the air in a country worn down by economic decline and relentless emigration in the 1950s. In that decade, more than half a million people voted with their feet and left the country. There was much to change, economically, socially and culturally in the country, but not many might have expected change to arrive quite so quickly. Yet various forces combined to produce quite sudden major changes that would touch Tony, his city, his country and the wider world.

The combined efforts of politician Sean Lemass and civil servant Ken Whitaker began to yield a tangible economic impact in Ireland. Lemass was elected Taoiseach in 1959, succeeding Éamon de Valera, who, many felt, had long passed his sell-by date as the political leader of Fianna Fáil, then – and until the general election in early 2011 – the largest party. De Valera was the party founder and first leader. The change represented by the more energetic, innovative and relatively younger Lemass resonated with other drivers of change. Earlier as a minister, Lemass had collaborated with Whitaker in

the promotion of the First Programme of Economic Expansion: this heralded the ending of the long-standing policy of economic protectionism
and opened up the economy to free trade and international investment,
major shifts, given the ideological roots of national self sufficiency in the
Fianna Fáil tradition. The old ways were changing and the future, it seemed,
was no longer inevitably based on more of the same.

Long a country of emigration and also linked to the wider world through
missionary activity and Irish involvement in the British empire, Ireland now
opened up to the world economically and in other ways. The Irish Army
undertook its first peacekeeping assignment in 1960, in the Congo. Also
in 1960 Aer Lingus joined the jet age with a service with Boeings on the
North Atlantic to New York and Boston. Princess Grace of Monaco – for-
merly the celebrated Hollywood actress Grace Kelly, and with strong Irish
roots – paid a high-impact state visit with her husband Prince Rainier in
1961. At the end of that year, a national television service, Teilifís Éireann,
later RTÉ (Raidio Teilifís Éireann), made its first broadcast.

And there were significant developments on the international stage. The
United States and the Soviet Union were then engaged in a struggle for
supremacy on many fronts in their 'Cold War' – an ideological struggle,
put simply, between communism and capitalism as economic and political models. In 1959 the Soviets had landed an unmanned spacecraft on the
moon, and in 1961 achieved a huge psychological and propaganda coup by
sending the first manned flight into space. The Americans were on the back
foot in the space race with their Cold War competitors, and it wasn't until
1966 that they had regained some prestige with their first manned space
flight, following this with the first landing on the moon in 1969.

In July 1962 RTÉ launched *The Late Late Show* with its chat-show-cum-
entertainment format. It played a huge part in opening up taboo issues and
sparking national debate, aided by the talents of its presenter and director
Gay Byrne, who continued to present the show for thirty-seven years. Some

of its most controversial moments related to coverage of matters to do with sexuality or Church–State relations.

John Fitzgerald Kennedy, the US President, visited Ireland in the summer of 1963, only a few months before his assassination in Dallas, Texas. JFK enjoyed a very special status in many Irish homes, with his image often hung alongside one or more images of the Pope or the Sacred Heart, a greatly venerated religious image in Catholic Ireland. And in November of the same year The Beatles – the Fab Four from Liverpool – came to Dublin to play two concerts in the Adelphi cinema on Abbey Street. This was a huge event and gave a dramatic glimpse of the new energy and tastes of the young people of the day.

Fine Gael published an important policy document for the party, *Towards a Just Society*, in 1965. The document was written by Declan Costello and appeared a year ahead of the fiftieth anniversary of the 1916 Rising. It was an interesting attempt to assert *social* as well as economic priorities in the national agenda. A new breed of socially aware journalism too was finding expression in *The Irish Times* and RTÉ. Michael Viney was a leading exponent of this committed and authoritative journalistic approach, while on television, *Seven Days*, an investigative current affairs programme, commenced broadcasting in September 1966.

The fiftieth anniversary of 1916 got off with a bang, thanks mainly to the IRA who blew up Nelson's Pillar, the column that stood tall in O'Connell Street near the General Post Office, commemorating Admiral Horatio Nelson. Or, more precisely, the IRA blew up half of it, the Irish army actually having to complete the job. While cosily familiar to most Dubliners, Nelson's departure, even in these circumstances, seems not to have been greatly regretted – the symbolism of a statue of a British admiral staring down on the populace was not lost on the citizenry of the day and there were not too many tears shed for the demise of this colonial relic.

The anniversary of the Rising gave a fillip to consciousness of republican and reforming agendas. In terms of social policy, housing problems were a major issue, especially in Dublin, and significant political protest crystallised around housing conditions. Housing provision for poorer families had been a running sore in the life of the city for over a century. Various large housing estates had been built for the working class in Marino, Drumcondra and Cabra by the new State in the 1920s and in other places later.[11] Yet there still remained in the 1960s a chronic shortage of suitable accommodation in Dublin, forcing many families to live in unsafe or unsuitable conditions. The city's unfortunate record of poor housing, stretching back into the nineteenth century, was still very much a live issue. Many families were caught between private landlords unwilling to accommodate children, and the public landlord, Dublin Corporation, that continued to be slow to face up to the level of unmet need. The city authorities relied on a form of rationing in response to the shortage of housing by restricting offers of tenancies to families with at least four children – this was the measure that Tony's mother had encountered in the early 1950s, and it was still in force over a decade later. Adding to the pressure were a number of incidents involving the collapse of inner-city tenement houses in 1963. In June of that year, two tragedies unfolded: in the first incident two adults were killed in the collapse of a tenement in Bolton Street, and a week or two later two children died in falling rubble from a collapsing tenement in Fenian Street.

There was an angry public reaction and the Dublin Corporation Housing Committee was forced to give overall priority to people living in dangerous accommodation. In the four-month period from June to September 1963, 367 'Dangerous Buildings Notices' that obliged families or single persons to leave dangerous property were served by Dublin Corporation. This was a far higher rate of such notices than in earlier periods. These emergency measures led to 900 families and 326 single persons being evacuated.[12]

It is clear that Dublin Corporation had had a wake-up call. The need for this wake-up call was linked to the fact that in the period 1956/57 to

1960/61 there had been a drop from 1,564 to 277 in the number of houses built by Dublin Corporation.[13]

By 1965, the pressure on the Corporation and the government was building further in relation to the city's housing issues. A Fine Gael TD, Richie Ryan, was among those strongly vocal on the housing question in Dublin – he was later the Minister for Finance who was mercilessly lampooned as 'Richie Ruin' by Frank Hall and his fellow satirists on *Hall's Pictorial Weekly,* a satirical programme on RTÉ television at the time. As Minister for Finance he might have opposed reforms requiring more spending, but as a backbencher he was prepared to highlight problems. In a Dáil budget debate, Ryan raised the housing issue, decrying policy failures that had left

10,000 families representing 40,000 people without a home to call their own and most of them with no prospect of having a home of their own within the next two years … What is done in the midst of all this absolutely unnecessary housing crisis? We have spent, within the past year, £20,000 on maintaining a disused army barracks [Griffith Barracks] at South Circular Road, Dublin, to house some 30 to 40 homeless families. But what do we find some members of this great housing committee doing to justify this? We find them engaging in propaganda suggesting that these families are problem families and are there through their own maladministration, because they are impossible families for whom one cannot do anything, because they are difficult families. What is the truth? The truth is that most of the fathers of the families in Griffith Barracks are in good employment and the only reason they cannot get any accommodation is that the private renters of property or rooms will not have children in flats. Again and again evictions take place in this city for no reason other than that young married couples have a child born to them and where such young are unable to get accommodation in their parents' houses they have no alternative, unless they have four children, but to take the road to Griffith Barracks and stay there until such time as the Corporation reach a position where they begin to house families of mother and father and three children, a situation which is shortly about to be reached.[14]

Among the many dreadful features of this housing situation was a bar on couples living together. A condition of accommodation in Griffith Barracks was that men could not share with their partners – they had to fend for themselves somewhere else. This reality began to come to public attention when, in August 1965, eighteen families protested and moved out to a tented encampment.[15] This was located on waste ground in North Great Charles Street, off Mountjoy Square, a few blocks away from Tony's home and a street or two away from his secondary school at O'Connell's. This move by the families was sparked by the eviction of eighteen husbands from the Griffith Barracks accommodation after the families had staged a twelve-day lock-in protest against the husbands being separated from their families and some of the mothers from their children.[16]

SCHOOL AND BEYOND

These events undoubtedly helped to shape the political awareness and motivation of the young Tony as he worked his way through the secondary school system. Jim Sheridan, Tony's schoolmate, recalls a harsh regime at secondary school with the Brothers. He himself decided to leave school after the Intermediate Certificate examination (equivalent to today's Junior Certificate) at sixteen years of age, when he discovered a more benign atmosphere in the world of work, and he chose to stay on in what had started out as a summer job. Tony stuck it out at O'Connell's and did his Leaving Certificate examinations.

After the Leaving Certificate, some of Tony's classmates were going to England to work for the summer. He decided to go too and also to apply for a place in University College Dublin (UCD), as some of the others were doing. He got his place on the Bachelor in Arts course, and the money from the summer job – in a Wall's ice cream factory in Acton in west London – gave him the means to manage the cost of going to university. Tony completed his Arts degree and then did his Higher Diploma in Education (HDip). This one-year, post-graduate course was a passport to a job as a secondary school teacher. In later years, Tony was coy about whether teaching was the career he really wanted – in one interview he let slip that he would have been interested in studying law.[17] At the time, however, teaching offered a job, which was a pretty important consideration for someone who had come from a background where economic security was paramount. Becoming a teacher was also a great gift to give his mother to make up for her own thwarted ambitions.

Tony was only twenty-two years old when his mother died in 1969, at the age of sixty-five. According to Noel, Tony was 'very traumatised' by her death. Apparently, he learned of it from a Garda who called to the door as the family had no telephone at the time and the hospital where she died – Blanchardstown – had no other means of contacting them. Ellen was a very religious woman and Tony had always wanted to take her to Lourdes in recognition of that, and in appreciation of all she had done for him; Lourdes shrine, of course, was hugely venerated by Irish Catholics of her era. But Tony didn't have the money to take her there, and, unfortunately, she died before savings from his salary as a teacher would have allowed him to fulfil that wish. He was sorry too that she didn't live to see his political successes according to Maureen O'Sullivan, an early political supporter from East Wall and Tony's longtime friend and political associate (and successor as TD). Maureen recalls the celebrations for Tony's first election being tinged with sadness; talking to Maureen in the midst of all the excitement and emotion, tears welled up in Tony as he recalled that his mother had not lived to see his victory.

TEACHER

As a teacher, Tony taught first during his HDip trainee year in the vocational school in Great Denmark Street. Vocational (technical) schools aimed, generally, to serve students who often had less academic ambitions than those in secondary schools, and who were typically from humbler backgrounds. This school, where Tony set out on his career as a teacher, was only a few doors up from Belvedere College, the Jesuit school that served the aspiring middle classes of Dublin. At the time almost none of the students at Belvedere came from its local area.

When the principal in Denmark Street sized up his new HDip student on first encounter, he offered a sceptical assessment as he compared the inclinations of his students with the youthful inexperience that Tony brought: 'I don't think you're going to be able for this' were his inspirational and reassuring words! One of Tony's students that year was Philip Boyd, who was later to become a friend through their shared involvement in community affairs and other connections. Philip says that the principal's fears were unfounded. Tony was able 'to keep a good amount of order', and he didn't need any theatrical gestures – the students just 'understood'. As Philip recalls, 'He could cut you with a look.' One day the students decided to poke some harmless fun at one of Tony's habits as a teacher – he would constantly pace back and forth across the top of the classroom. The students trained their eyes on him and their heads swivelled in unison from left to right and back in an exaggerated fashion, following his movement. This went on for a few minutes until Tony 'copped' it, and abandoned the habit forever. Even as a student teacher, Tony seems to have displayed a competence and canniness that people underestimated at their peril. He already had a sense of authority and 'cop on' that would stand him in good stead in later years.

After qualifying, Tony's first job was in Coláiste Mhuire, a Christian Brothers' school on Parnell Square, where Irish was the language of instruction. It was close to the vocational school in Denmark Street and also to Belvedere College where, by coincidence, Tony's brother, Noel, had been hired as a teacher of Irish.

During that first year of teaching, Tony took part in a seven-day march from Dublin to Cork, sponsored by the *United Irishman* newspaper with the support of Sinn Féin, to highlight the plight of six longterm Republican prisoners in Britain. For a teacher, the march conveniently took place during school holidays – it was scheduled to end with a mass rally in the centre of Cork on Christmas Day 1970.[18]

After a year at Coláiste Mhuire, Tony moved south of the Liffey to the celebrated Christian Brothers' school in Synge Street, off the South Circular Road. His students there included John Crown, later to become a Professor of Oncology, a vocal critic in the media of the shortcomings in the health services, and a UCD Senator in the 2011 Seanad elections. Tony was eventually to lose his job in 'Synger', seemingly because of his connections to republican politics which did not go down well with the Brothers there. The incident that apparently brought matters to a head was a court appearance that Liz Doyle, a friend from his Sinn Féin days (see Chapter 2), believes was linked to the 'acquisition' of a car intended for use in support of the work of the Dublin Housing Action Committee. Tony turned up in court with his co-accused, fearing the worst. But, as it turned out, their bacon was saved by a miraculous turn of events. They were being represented by a young barrister very early in his career, who was to become the very well-known Senior Counsel, Patrick McEntee. McEntee was whiling away the time in court waiting for the case to be heard when one of the intervening cases turned out to require a good knowledge of Latin, something that the judge did not possess. The eager young McEntee offered his services as translator and the case proceeded smoothly. To show his appreciation, the judge announced 'case dismissed' when McEntee's case involving Tony and his friend was called!

Tony's luck was in for a second time in relation to losing his job in Synge Street. Brother Ó Donabháin, the principal in 'Synger', did not approve of Tony's politics and decided to let him go. His parting words were along the lines: 'You're not our sort.' But Tony's teaching career was rescued by his colleague, Brother Keegan. Tony had applied for a post in another Christian Brothers' secondary school, Coláiste Eoin in Stillorgan, where Irish was the language of instruction. When the principal there, Brother Ó Dugáin, phoned Synge Street to get a reference, Brother Ó Donabháin happened not to be in the school on the day. Brother Keegan took the call and gave Tony a glowing reference, thus landing him the job. Ó Dugáin came to value Tony's teaching talent and had less dislike of his politics. Tony taught in the school right up until his election as a Teachta Dála (TD) when he took leave from teaching. He taught history to Leaving Cert level and French to Junior Cert, both through Irish. Looking back, it seems that he did not regret too much what turned out to be the premature ending of his teaching career. In 1995, thirteen years into his fulltime career as a politician, he reflected on life as a teacher: 'To be perfectly honest, twelve years is enough for anyone,' he said.[19]

But his students did not necessarily share this self-assessment of Tony and the business of teaching. According to former students in Coláiste Eoin, Tony was an 'inspirational' teacher. His approach to teaching history was to get his students to engage in discussion and reflection, and not just in rote learning. Instead of standard school textbooks, he used the more scholarly and detailed book by the historian FSL Lyons, *Ireland since the Famine*, as his course text. 'Tony Gregory was the best teacher I ever had,' stated Colm Mac Eochaidh, Senior Counsel, who helped to trigger the establishment of the Flood tribunal; he was also a campaigner on environmental planning issues and a Fine Gael Dáil candidate in Dublin South East in the 2002 election.[20]

Another pupil, Leslie O'Neill, first encountered Tony when he became a student in Coláiste Eoin in 1971. He wrote a glowing endorsement of Tony as a teacher just after Tony was elected to the Dáil, highlighting some of the strengths that Tony would also demonstrate in politics.

He taught History and French and if he is as good a politician as he was a teacher, we should be hearing a lot more about him. In school there was a general rule that if you caused trouble in class, you were sent to the head brother, to have your punishment dished out. But with Tony it was different. He always said that if you did not want to learn, then you could either leave or study somewhere else so long as you did not cause any trouble. He was one of the few teachers who treated us as equals and with a high degree of respect. His history classes were something to be cherished. He was a teacher who believed in not only teaching the subject, but debating, questioning and arguing the subject in great depth. He never talked from the top of the class, he always sat among us like another pupil, listening and speaking just like everybody else. The number of times that our classes ran over time was unbelievable. I remember one particular day we stayed well over an hour past normal school finishing time. Even other teachers had trouble getting him out of the class. We were so enthralled by this man, that we debated history during the following class (much to the annoyance of the teacher in charge). I hope Tony Gregory never retires from teaching because he is one of the finest teachers I have ever met ... He was extremely hard-working.[21]

It seems, however, that Tony's vision of the role of teachers did not extend to marking homework, yet, he was ambitious for his students and was very proud of the academic achievements of his protégés. He greatly valued each honours A grade they achieved in the Leaving Cert. As the teacher, he saw himself as partly sharing in their success − this appealed to the competitive streak in him. Among his students were Liam Ó Maonlaí, later of the rock group Hot House Flowers and also a distinguished solo performer, and Aengus Ó Snodaigh, who was to be elected as a Sinn Féin TD in 2007 for Dublin South Central, and who was a member of the Sinn Féin negotiating team at critical Peace Process talks. Ó Snodaigh recalls there being 'great debates in his classes'.[22]

Though Tony taught French and history, and had taken history as a main subject in his degree, remarkably he had not studied it at school. Instead, he had taught himself history at home in order to take it independently as a Leaving Cert subject, earning an honours grade under his own tutelage.[23] In this, there is a telling glimpse of the independence, determination and dedication that Tony could later bring to other projects.

***

In many senses, Tony Gregory lived his whole life in a village. He certainly grew up in a village. It was a village marked out by the Royal Canal and a number of main roads criss-crossing the central-city area. From the age of twelve, he lived in the same house in that village, in Sackville Gardens, and the previous twelve years had been spent in the flat in Charleville Avenue, just around the corner. The schools he attended were all located within a stone's throw of his front door. And later, as his work and life took him outside this village, he based himself and his work there and always returned to it.

There were many influences on the young Tony as he moved ever closer to a career devoted to politics. His father's political stories, his mother's commitment to education, the environs of his 'village', the hard times and housing challenges the family had encountered, the signs of poverty all around his locality, the media coverage of injustices in the city and nationally, the virtual educational apartheid that he had encountered repeatedly both as student and teacher, his interest in history and politics, the national celebrations for the fiftieth anniversary of the 1916 Rising, his exposure to political ideas through Sinn Féin. All of these forged a powerful commitment in the young Tony to social and political change.

CHAPTER 2

• • • • • •

From Sinn Féin to Community Politics

Tony recalled in an interview how he and a friend dropped in to the Sinn Féin offices in 1963, when he was sixteen, and asked to join the IRA (Irish Republican Army). They were told to come back in a year. True to form, Tony did come back; even then he was consistent and true to his beliefs. He joined Sinn Féin and the IRA. Tony had been a teenage member of the FCA (Fórsaí Cosanta Áitiúil/Local Defence Forces, a branch of the army), in a company whose commanding officer was Dermot Ring, a neighbour from nearby Clonmore Terrace. Noel recalls Tony knocking on Dermot Ring's door to resign his membership of the FCA, an event that Noel presumes coincided with his joining the republican movement.

A few years later, as a university student, Tony helped to found the UCD Republican Club, whose establishment had long been resisted by the college authorities. Yet John Lynch, a friend of Tony's from school and the neighbourhood, recalls Garret FitzGerald – then a lecturer in the Department of Economics at UCD, later to be leader of Fine Gael and Taoiseach, and already a high-profile figure in Irish life – chatting with them at their Republican Club stall during Freshers' week where they were making the case for recognition by the college authorities. Lynch recalls FitzGerald commenting along the lines of 'Well done, lads', obviously approving of political activity among students, whatever its focus. A sustained campaign for recognition of the club eventually bore fruit. By November 1968, the UCD Republican Club was up and running and could claim sixty-four members.[1] This, of course, was before the outbreak of the Troubles in the North in 1969 and the gradual polarising of southern opinion on the northern question.

According to Noel, Tony was active around this time too in the Dublin Housing Action Committee (DHAC), which had been launched publicly in May 1967 to highlight housing problems in the city; it was part of a set of local housing action committees across the country. There was certainly a major housing crisis in the city, exemplified, among other things, by the aforementioned collapse of tenements in Bolton Street and Fenian Street a few years earlier. In January 1969, when President Éamon De Valera addressed a specially convened meeting of the Dáil in Dublin's Mansion House to mark the fiftieth anniversary of the First Dáil held in that same venue, his speech was heckled by veteran republican Joe Clarke, protesting against the imprisonment of Dennis Dennehy, a DHAC activist who had been squatting in a property in Mountjoy Square in the north inner city. DHAC was very adept in the use of high-profile actions calculated to gain publicity for their cause, which was to get housing for people in dire need. Tactics included pickets, marches, occupations and squatting. It also published at least one issue of a newsletter, *Squatter*, in June 1969. One of its main messages was to advocate the occupation of empty property by homeless families.[2] DHAC was led by Sinn Féin activists, but non-republicans were also involved.[3] Among these were the Jesuit priest Fr Michael Sweetman and the Dominican priest Fr Austin Flannery, who was also strongly associated with other liberal causes, one of which was the very active Irish branch of the anti-apartheid movement, a highly effective international movement relentlessly opposing the racist apartheid regime that ran South Africa from 1948 to 1984. While the assertive approach of DHAC gained a lot of public attention, by mid-1970 it had begun to run out of steam due to two factors: developments in the North of Ireland were drawing away the attention of Sinn Féin people and, badly stung by its robust and attention-grabbing occupations, marches and other such tactics, the State authorities took a harder line against DHAC actions.

By early 1970, a split within Sinn Féin on a range of issues, including abstentionism (a policy of not taking up seats in parliament when elected) and the leftist policies of the leadership led to the establishment of what became known as the 'Provisional Sinn Féin/IRA'. Tony remained with what became 'Official Sinn Féin' in order to distinguish it from the breakaway group. Tony rose through the ranks very quickly. In March 1971 Tony had a letter published in *The Irish Times*, signed as Anthony Gregory and giving his home address. In it he highlighted Sinn Féin's anti-EEC (European Economic Community) position in the national debate about possible Irish membership – the EEC was the forerunner of today's European Union (EU).

On 9 August 1971, Brian Faulkner, Leader of the Unionist party and Northern Ireland Prime Minister, introduced internment of IRA members, meaning that the government took the power to detain indefinitely and without trial anyone they selected. Tony was in Belfast on the day internment without trial was suddenly enforced by the British army as they raided nationalist areas to 'lift' their targets. It turned out to be a hamfisted and poorly planned action. The measure was designed to curtail the IRA, but it failed in two ways: firstly, the authorities lacked accurate intelligence and thus many 'innocent' people were lifted; secondly, the crude nature of the exercise served to alienate many people in nationalist communities and served as a very effective recruiting device for the IRA. However, that is an appraisal in retrospect. On the day, the raw urge to escape the dragnet was the urgent imperative. Local women banged bin lids to warn of the arrival of the British army vehicles used in the raids. Tony was staying with republican contacts in the city and the challenge was to prevent him being lifted. The story goes that his contact managed to secure a white coat from a local butcher, which Tony duly donned. It was then 'arranged' for an ambulance to convey him in full regalia to Central Station, where Tony boarded the train for Dublin and freedom – no doubt dutifully handing back the white coat for return to its rightful owner. Pádraig Yeates, then a republican activist and later an *Irish Times* journalist, recalls having met Tony briefly in Belfast around that time – he also recalls making good his own escape from the internment dragnet on a Dublin train and the palpable tension among a number of similarly motivated passengers until the train had crossed the border.

Although a relatively young man at that point, Tony had sufficient status within the organisation to be charged with giving an Easter Sunday oration at the Republican Plot in Dean's Grange cemetery in 1972.[4] In the speech, Tony was reported to have said that it was 'as important to vote "No" in the [then upcoming] referendum on [joining] the EEC as it was to resist British troops in the North.' For a long time, Sinn Féin regarded the EEC as a threat to Irish sovereignty, hence the position that Tony took in the speech.

Despite his growing stature in the organisation, Tony was to resign from Official Sinn Féin later that year. He said later he did so in frustration over the various ideological splits that began to dominate the organisation. The 'movement' was riven with tension and division on the direction it should take on a range of issues – on the balance of political and military influence, on whether it should strive to be part of, or lead, a broader movement as opposed to following a more traditional model for a left-wing party, on the issue of cessation of violence versus a more activist approach to military intervention. Inevitably, perhaps, an extraordinary degree of intrigue and distrust developed among members. Many reacted by leaving, Tony included. In a later interview with Proinsias Mac Aonghusa, Tony said he had left the party within a year of changes that began happening around 1972, changes which he saw as being orchestrated by people who would not join the party but wanted to influence it.[5] At times, the conflict split into feuds which claimed some victims and left many others fearing for their lives.

Some of those who left gathered around Seamus Costello, who had been dismissed from the movement by court-martial, having once been one of its most powerful and charismatic figures. When Costello formed the Irish Republican Socialist Party (IRSP) in 1974, he asked Tony to join. Tony was reluctant, feeling that he had given his all to the Officials and had very little to show for it. Costello persuaded him at least to help build the numbers by signing up.

Seamus Costello was a complex figure in the republican movement. He was very popular among the rank and file, but not with all elements of the leadership. He was identified as broadly hard-line in the use of 'armed struggle' to advance political aims. At the remarkably young age of seventeen he found himself the leader of an active-service unit in the ill-fated IRA Border campaign of the 1950s. Being given this status so young hinted at the leadership qualities that he would demonstrate in many contexts in later life. In the late 1950s, Costello was interned for two years, a time he later described as 'my university days'. While in favour of the use of arms, he was also extremely committed to on-the-ground activism in relation to the political concerns of ordinary people. He built a republican presence in local politics in County Wicklow from his base in Bray and succeeded in being elected as a member of Wicklow County Council and Bray Urban District Council (1967), finally topping the poll in both in 1974. Electoral success was the result of well-organised effort and clear identification with local organisations, such as tenants associations and the Bray Trades Council.[6] Tony reviewed the organisational reasons for Costello's electoral success in a county where for a long time previously the Sinn Féin organisation had been effectively dormant:

Seamus led and organised an extremely efficient four-week campaign, distributing 75,000 pieces of literature, 3,000 posters, with 15 people working every night. Sinn Féin was the only party to canvass every house and hold numerous public meetings.[7]

Clearly, Tony drew inspiration for his own later electoral efforts from the model he describes here.

Costello had impact and earned respect even from people who did not share his views. One such example is Noel Browne, who attended an invited conference in the United States in which Costello was a participant. Browne was very impressed by Costello and what he had to say.[8] Costello had a great gift for communication and he saw the importance of reaching a wider audience with his message. He was bitterly opposed to the traditional Sinn Féin policy of abstentionism and worked for its abolition – he saw abstentionism as a barrier to winning wider support; this was one of the key issues in the split that led to the formation of the breakaway Provisional Sinn Féin, who supported abstention. Costello had remained with the Officials, but was ultimately expelled, which had led him, in 1974, to founding the IRSP, and, more covertly, a military wing, the Irish National Liberation Army (INLA). Costello was assassinated on a Dublin street in 1977 at the age of thirty-eight. Without his guiding hand, the INLA gradually became synonymous with indiscriminate mayhem.

In a *Hot Press* interview towards the end of his life, and published after he died, Tony says that, for the record, he had 'agreed to join [Costello's new party, the IRSP] on paper but [had] never got involved with the political organisation itself.'[9] When Costello was shot dead in October 1977, it marked a turning point in Tony's political direction: 'I severed all connections, more or less, with any sort of political organisation then at that time.'

According to Noel, Tony was devastated by Costello's death. But in practical terms it meant that Tony was now committed to a political path outside political parties. Although Tony did not make much subsequent reference to it, there is some evidence that he did have some slight involvement with the Socialist Labour Party (SLP), a party founded by the trade union activist Matt Merrigan and the politician Noel Browne in 1977. It grew, in part, from left-wing members of the Labour Party and succeeded in getting one TD elected, Noel Browne. A strongly anti-republican speech by Noel Browne in May 1978 must surely have alienated Tony, apart from any other reservations he might have had about links to yet another political party. However, it appears that some in the local north inner-city branch of the SLP still actively entertained the hope that he would stand as a candidate for that party in the north inner city in the 1979 council elections. But looking back, Maureen O'Sullivan believes that this was 'never a runner'. In his book on Noel Browne, John Horgan reports, on the basis of SLP branch minutes, that Tony resigned from the SLP in April 1979[10] – this was as the party descended into disarray partly as a result of the increasingly idiosyncratic style of its highest profile politician, Noel Browne. By 1982, the SLP was wound up.

MICK RAFFERTY AND FERGUS McCABE: THE ROAD TO COMMUNITY POLITICS

Mick Rafferty recalls a knock on the door of his flat in Mount Street, on Dublin's south side in the early 1970s. It was a young Australian, Jim Ryan, who wanted him to become involved in the Dublin Tutorial Group – a group of students, mainly, who were running an educational and recreational project for children from Sheriff Street, the community where Mick had spent his teenage years.

Mick had lived in Ballyfermot until he was ten years old, and then moved with his family to Sheriff Street flats. His father was a 'button man' on the docks – dockers were hired on a daily basis as shipping traffic in the port required, and the button man hired the men needed each day, a powerful position. Mick remembers being with his father on the morning of the last 'read' on the docks, the last time the old system of hiring was used before containers replaced human labour; containerisation signalled the end of the docks as an important source of income for local men and essentially heralded the mechanisation of work previously done by an army of dockers.

Mick left school at fourteen and began his apprenticeship as an electrician. In his teenage years, he was drawn to ideas about how the world could be a better place, beginning his exploration in Christianity and later joining the socialist Connolly Youth Movement with another local lad. He remembers as a teenager going to the library to look for a book about fixing motorbikes and happening on a book introducing the history of philosophy. This chance find made a big impression on him: the book argued that the shape of society should reflect its purpose. In his Christian phase, and well beyond, Mick continued to believe that the shape of society should reflect a higher Christian or political purpose.

Fergus McCabe came from a different social background. His father was a post office supervisor. Fergus grew up off the Navan Road in what are now the inner suburbs of Dublin, just beyond the working class area of Cabra. He went to school with the Jesuits in Belvedere College on Denmark Street. Fergus's time in Belvedere led on to a lifelong commitment to the inner city when he became a volunteer youth leader in the Belvedere Newsboys Club, later to become the Belvedere Youth Club. The club had been founded in the early 1900s by past students from Belvedere College. In his teens his thinking also moved, like Mick's, from religion to politics, and he became remarkably well read in international history for a schoolboy. He was influenced by the social movements of his day. His love of folk music also introduced him to the causes of human rights supported by many folk-song writers. He joined the Anti-Apartheid movement and took part in the protest against the all-white South African Springbok rugby team when they played Ireland in a very controversial rugby match in Lansdowne Road in 1966. Fergus was still at school, and was apprehensive that his picketing might not go down well with the Jesuit priests from Belvedere if they spotted him on the protest; he was relieved to discover that one of his fellow picketers was Séamus Ó Tuathail, a republican, a one-time editor of the *United Irishman* and a teacher of Irish in Belvedere at the time, who later went on to be a barrister and supporter of Tony's. The young Fergus figured that the presence on the protest of one of his teachers gave him valuable political cover should he be hauled in to explain himself by the formidable Prefect of Studies (principal) who could do a very good line in scary.

Influenced by his experiences in Belvedere and after a history degree in UCD, Fergus trained in professional social work, also at UCD, with the support of a grant from the Eastern Health Board psychiatric service. His talent had been spotted by Professor Ivor Browne, then Chief Psychiatrist in the Eastern Health Board and Professor of Psychiatry at UCD, who encouraged and supported his interest in community development in the north inner city; Browne recognised that this assignment would make good use of Fergus's prior knowledge of the area. Browne was a colourful character who liked to relax in traffic jams by playing his tin whistle. He readily abandoned the narrow scope of conventional psychiatry and saw that poverty and powerlessness were the seed-bed of many mental health problems; he believed that psychiatry should be concerned with fostering healthier social conditions where human beings could thrive: in other words, it should be treating causes as well as symptoms. Accordingly, Browne had founded the community development division in the UCD Department of Psychiatry and this eventually was to become the Irish Foundation for Human Development. Ivor Browne and Paddy Walley, a key member of the Foundation, agreed that the mental health of the local north inner-city community collectively was inextricably bound up with the social conditions of that community. This made community development an appropriate technique for use by a local mental health social worker, since community development sought to instil the energy, skills and confidence in local communities to organise in order to express their needs and priorities. Fergus devoted a lot of energy to organising tenant committees in inner-city flat complexes. Browne and Walley saw this as a logical step based on their successful earlier experiences supporting community development in Derry and Ballyfermot.

Mick agreed to become involved in the Dublin Tutorial Group. This re-connection with the Sheriff Street community eventually led to his becoming Secretary of the local Community Association. He soon discovered the harsh realities of political organising. It was not easy to arouse interest in the objectively important and major issues, such as a planned motorway through the area or unemployment, but, he said, 'You could fill a hall on the issue of piped television'– the forerunner of cable TV, piped television offered access to a range of TV channels beyond the then staple diet of RTÉ, and also high-quality reception far superior to that which might be obtained by the ubiquitous TV aerials on the roofs of houses and flats complexes. As part of his committee work, Mick helped to run a week-long community festival in the Sheriff Street area in 1974, complete with bonny babies and the release of doves.

During that festival, Mick Rafferty and Fergus McCabe met each other for the first time. Unknown to Tony and to themselves, this meeting was to prove very influential in all their lives and eventually in the political future of Tony Gregory. Fergus explained to Mick the development work he was doing, organising tenants groups mostly in and around Summerhill. They had both heard of something similar going on in Ballybough and East Wall. Together, they decided to organise a conference for all the local groups to be held in Lourdes Hall in Sean McDermott Street. Mick says that this meeting was where they first met Tony. The meeting, in time-honoured fashion, agreed to form a committee and this led, in turn, to the formation of the North Central Community Council (NCCC) in February 1975. This was to serve as a coordinating body for emerging tenant and community groups. Tony was its secretary. An early achievement was preparing a plan for submission to the Corporation for the 1976 review of the Dublin Development Plan in November 1976.[11] Their plan was prepared with technical assistance from the Irish Foundation for Human Development; its Director, Ivor Browne, recalls being invited to north inner-city Dublin and agreeing 'to offer our expertise in planning and guidance' and to help develop a 'counter-proposal' to the Corporation's own plan.[12] Mick recalls that the analysis by the Foundation was very influential in developing his own thinking – the first time he heard of the term 'inner city' and of the concept of 'multiple disadvantage' was in discussion with Paddy Walley and others working with the Foundation, which also had a presence in Ballyfermot and Derry.

While Tony, Mick and Fergus drew on wide experience and knowledge, much of their focus was necessarily on local issues – promoting local development, creating opportunities for local people, highlighting shortfalls and injustices in provision, and opposing undesirable projects. One prominent example of the latter was opposition to a plan for a motorway through the area; in May 1979 Tony was co-signatory of a letter to *The Irish Times* from Sackville Gardens, Clonliffe and District Anti-Motorway committee outlining the reasons for opposing this. The objections were manifold: the alleged benefits of any motorway would accrue to suburban dwelling car owners; the economic and social costs would be lumbered on inner-city communities whose area would be divided, degraded or destroyed to facilitate the motorways; in their construction and operation, motorways would wreak havoc on the quality of life in inner-city communities, and on the architectural and cultural heritage of the city.

Nor was it ever a case of expecting others to do the work. Tony, Fergus and Mick were willing to roll up their sleeves in various ways themselves. Being a teacher, Tony had more spare time than the others to deal with the demands of being secretary. By December 1976, Tony, as secretary, could claim that the NCCC represented twelve community and tenants associations in the north inner city. While the NCCC wanted a clear focus on big issues, such as the motorway or unemployment, Tony also proved skilful at identifying 'smaller' issues on which it might be possible to make some tangible progress more quickly. One such issue was youth facilities. Tony produced evidence that the area received a lower share of Corporation grants for youth provision than other areas, despite its objective deprivation.

An early battleground for the NCCC, therefore, was to win control of local summer projects to provide summertime activities for local children and young people. Since 1973 these had been run by the Catholic Youth Council (CYC), which operated under the auspices of the Catholic Archdiocese of Dublin, and the NCCC wanted the grants received from the Corporation for these projects to go to local groups under local control rather than to the CYC who employed outside students. In 1976, the NCCC succeeded in securing support for one trial project under local management: the Ballybough Summer Project ran successfully in July and August that year and employed one worker, Philip Boyd from Clonliffe Avenue. He was an activist and, as already mentioned, a former student of Tony's in his HDip year. By the following year, NCCC had overcome opposition from the Corporation and local councillors to achieve a set of eight local projects with eight locally recruited workers.[13]

This battle over summer projects foreshadowed a general theme in NCCC's strategy: NCCC wanted more local involvement and accountability in the operation of local provision. But if the state system were to accommodate this demand, it had to engage with a local partner to be held accountable for the use of public money. It was tempting for NCCC to offer to play the role of partner and thereby be seen to deliver resources to the local community, which they did. But there was a price to be paid – it meant NCCC becoming a project manager, thus risking diversion from the single and fearless focus that NCCC had previously had on political activism. This was an interesting first step for the NCCC group in becoming drawn into the mainstream political process.

Another key battle, perhaps, in establishing NCCC and testing Tony's political mettle was the resistance they mounted to the announcement by the Dublin City Council on 1 August 1978 that the Council had decided to demolish the tenement buildings in the Summerhill–Gardiner Street area. Within six weeks, Tony, as secretary of the NCCC, claimed at a news conference that 81 percent of local residents surveyed in the three localities affected wanted to be re-housed in the area.[14] At a seminar organised by the Irish Planning Institute a month later, Tony was reported as calling planners 'vandals in pinstripe suits'. He was also reported as lambasting Dublin Corporation officials for having failed to deliver proper maintenance services to inner-city tenants, and for planning the demolition of these flats without any plan to re-house the four thousand people affected.

Politically, Tony Gregory was a pragmatist. He retained a lifelong affinity with republicanism, yet he forged his closest political alliance with Fergus McCabe and Mick Rafferty, who came from another perspective on the issue of unity of the Republic and the North of Ireland. They were followers of the then quite exotic 'two nations' theory on partition; this theory opposed nationalist notions of the inevitability and moral imperative of a united Ireland. By separate pathways, Mick and Fergus had begun to adopt this view from the early 1970s. But for all their distinctive views on 'the North', Fergus's and Mick's commitment to issues closer to home made it possible to find common ground with Tony, even if this produced an unlikely political *ménage à trois*.

For Fergus, another area of difference with Tony was Fergus's support for the European Community. Fergus considered Europe as having a liberating influence on Irish politics and social policy, whereas Tony was strongly opposed to the erosion of national sovereignty that, he felt, European integration involved. Fergus's self-tutored political formation, his wide reading, his training in history, his admiration of figures such as Martin Luther King, Nelson Mandela and Mahatma Gandhi had led to his having a very internationalist outlook and an attitude that every just cause had to be seen as part of one great international struggle. From Fergus's vantage point, local conflicts could become too narrow and parochial in motivation and outlook, and could sometimes too easily tip into expressing exclusionary instincts, in which ultimately one side laid claim to being 'better' than the other without proper attention to the injustices both sides actually shared in reality, as in the working-class poverty shared across the sectarian divide in Northern Ireland.

However, the three of them managed to work closely together over the whole of Tony's political career, without once their divergent views on the 'national question' (or Europe) causing any turbulence. Mick recalls a discussion early in their political relationship in which the three of them agreed 'to bracket the North', and his memory is that they specifically used those words; they agreed too that any 'great injustice' could allow them to revisit this sidelining of the Northern question. The working relationship even survived the Hunger Strike period in 1981 when republican prisoners used the weapon of hunger strike to oppose the Thatcher government's policy in the United Kingdom of refusing to treat republican prisoners as political prisoners. The death of ten republican prisoners on hunger strike in Northern prisons caused major shock-waves in politics on the island and achieved huge media attention world-wide. Republicans hung black flags from lampposts all over the country in support of the hunger strike and in memory of those who died, and these flags became a powerful symbol of the heavy political tension that filled the air. There is some suggestion that Tony flirted with lending his name to efforts to seek the support of the Dublin dockers for the hunger strikers – this would have been a powerful economic and political weapon – but the effort fizzled out, thus relieving any possible stress or split on this issue in the ranks of Camp Gregory.[15]

The three activists had come to a similar position by different paths. Tony, Fergus and Mick shared adherence to broadly socialist principles and a common commitment to improving *social* conditions, especially in the inner city. Socialism, as they saw it, was about fairness in the balance between resources and need, with the distribution of resources being based on need rather than greed. This fairness was to be the over-riding economic and social principle in their vision. And there were long-standing grounds for concern about social conditions in the inner city, conditions which meant that local people bore a very unequal burden in terms of unemployment, housing distress and educational neglect. The three also shared a conviction that local people from the inner city had to exert extra pressure to be heeded by those with power and influence. These people had been ignored too long – and silent too long. As Fergus put it in an interview in *The Irish Times* in 1980 (after Tony's election as a councillor):[16]

> You can make the best reasoned argument in the world to them, but if you have not got muscle they will not give a damn. The only way to get even small changes is by being a nuisance.

In the same interview, Fergus noted that he had recently watched Charles Haughey on television arguing the need for people to tighten their belts economically. 'That was a laugh – coming from him', he commented, a comment with special resonance given what was to come down the tracks almost two years later when Haughey came to Summerhill Parade to negotiate Tony's support for his election as Taoiseach.

ENTERING COMMUNITY POLITICS

> 'Do you not get it, lads? The Irish are the blacks of Europe. And Dubliners are the blacks of Ireland. And the Northside Dubliners are the blacks of Dublin.'

> Jimmy Rabbitte in the film *The Commitments* (1991)

Jimmy Rabbitte's wit struck a chord with all Dubliners who watched Alan Parker's wonderful film, *The Commitments*. But residents of Dublin's north inner city might have added an extra line: 'And the Dubliners from the north inner city are the blacks of the Northside.' They lived in a compact yet hidden zone close to the heart of the capital, a population long cut off by a social apartheid from the mainstream of Irish life. It was very much that sense of marginalisation that drove Tony Gregory in his search for social justice for the inner-city areas whose deprivation and disadvantage scandalised him in the 1960s, 1970s and beyond.

These levels of deprivation had not come out of the blue, but arose from a situation of long-term neglect. Despite being close physically to the heartbeat of life in the capital, the north inner city had, in fact, long been a neglected after-thought in political terms. For more than a century, this zone had been a by-word in deprivation, and the slum conditions in this and similar parts of Dublin had achieved international notoriety. Writing in the mid-nineteenth century, Friedrich Engels, the wealthy British industrialist and collaborator of Karl Marx, wrote that the 'poorer districts of Dublin are among the most hideous and repulsive to be seen in the world ... and the filth, the uninhabitableness [sic] of the houses and the neglect of the streets surpass all description.'[17]

Long after it disappeared in the 1920s, the 'Monto' – a red light district in the north inner city – became the subject of a playful and popular song in the repertoire of the iconic folk group, The Dubliners, from the 1960s. But the large-scale prostitution associated with the Monto was truly no laughing matter; it was actually a serious threat to public health. The death rate from venereal disease in Dublin in 1916 was almost twice the rate for London and close to three times that for Belfast.[18] Thirty-five years earlier, a colonel commanding a British regiment based in Dublin had testified that over 43 percent of his men who were not married had been incapacitated for duty due to venereal disease. The picture of ill health in general was even bleaker in the area, thanks largely to unsanitary conditions. Death rates for Dublin in 1871 were 36 per 1,000 compared to rates of 24 for London, 22 for Glasgow or 21 for Edinburgh.[19]

The social history of Dublin from the mid-1800s to the mid-1900s and beyond reveals a consistent picture of neglect and of sluggish responses to the predicament of the city's poor. Prosperous Dublin could afford to ignore impoverished Dublin, except when problems boiled over so as to affect the more fortunate. And it was not even the case that a native government (from 1922) went on to make the necessary changes to transform the fortunes of the area. Monto was indeed cleaned up, but that was mostly due to the efforts of Frank Duff, the formidable founder of the Catholic lay organisation, the Legion of Mary, (as well as to the loss of trade occasioned by the departure of British garrisons) than to anything done by the new government.

As Tony entered the sphere of community politics and began his work in this part of the city in the mid-1970s, the indicators of neglect and deprivation were no less stark. The inner city was further worn down, in turn, by de-industrialisation, dereliction and de-population. Changes in labour practices, begun after the Second World War, gradually led inexorably to the closure of the docks, or more precisely the closure of most jobs in the port. Factories in the area – many with household names – began to close down or de-camp to suburban locations. Most of the 311 derelict sites in the city in 1978 were located within the canal ring circling the inner city, and mostly these were on the north side.[20]

Tony recognised that changes to the economic and social conditions of the north inner city would come only when local people affected by the issues pushed for them. Accordingly, he built his community base there, working outwards from his own street. He began by organising the Sackville Gardens Residents Association, and through that grouping he became involved in wider local networks and efforts. And throughout all his work, Tony was clear that the issues of the inner city reflected a wider set of challenges in Irish society. He might have been local in his concerns, but he was certainly not parochial. An extract from one of his early public communications with a political message – a letter to *The Irish Times* on 3 March 1978 in his personal capacity from his home address – underlines this point:

It is important to state that Dublin's inner city holds no monopoly on poverty and injustice. The inner city possibly suffers its most acute levels but that inequality and injustice are mirrored throughout Irish society.

In his work, his recreation and his politics, Tony devoted a lot of his energy to the betterment of young inner-city people, most especially those who were disadvantaged. Tony was very conscious that for those children there were very limited opportunities for holidays away from the city that other children might be able to take for granted. Around 1977, the opportunity to develop a holiday centre for inner-city kids in Cavan emerged. A project that opened up the countryside to inner-city kids would inevitably have a special place in Tony's heart, given his own wonderful memories of childhood holidays with his mother's people in County Offaly. Critical also was that the project would operate under the management of residents and professionals active in the inner city, which meant it would be close the realities of life there. The plan was to develop a holiday centre in a former boarding school that had been closed in 1972, and the premises were granted to the project on an initial ten-year lease formalised in 1979 by the Norbertine religious order that had run the school as part of the work of their abbey. The gift was channelled to community interests in the north inner city through Vincent Bolton, a local youth worker and former member of the order. Bolton remained close to his former abbot, Kevin Smith, and through the stories he relayed about life in the inner city and his work there, and about the success of holidays for inner-city youngsters he had helped organise in the Cavan Centre at Kilnacrott for the Belvedere Youth Club, Bolton had sown the seed in Smith's mind that such a gesture would be a worthwhile step. Tony was credited with being the project's founder, although this was a slight fudge, given both the background and the fact that he joined the committee shortly after its inception. He was, however, certainly a loyal activist for the project over his lifetime, remaining its chair until his death. As in everything he embraced, Tony was wholehearted about his involvement in the project. It was not just a matter of chairing meetings, he spent many weekends down at the centre cleaning, painting, building – whatever had to be done. By 1984, all the renovation and development efforts had produced a spanking new facility, much to the pride of all involved.

ELECTIONS

Tony stood for election for the Dublin City Council in 1979, the first time he dipped his toe in electoral waters. Looking back on his decision to stand, Tony said he was motivated by the low visibility in his locality of those politicians then serving as councillors, the latest crop of whom at that time had been elected in 1974.

At that point, there were six non-party candidates among the forty-five councillors elected to Dublin City Council. One was an old stager – the long-standing Independent Frank Sherwin, aged seventy-four. He was a veteran of the War of Independence and the Civil War and had been heavily involved in Fianna Fáil before falling out with the party over not being nominated as a Dáil candidate. He then had a number of early failed attempts in Dáil elections, but finally won a seat in a by-election in 1957 in the three-seater Dublin North Central with just over four thousand first preferences and a third of the vote. Sherwin held the seat in the 1961 general election, taking the second seat in what was by then a four-seater constituency on the first count. But it was downhill after that. He could only muster 1,615 votes in the next election in 1965. Sherwin's electoral history is relevant to Tony's story in that it proves that Independents in this constituency (the same one that would later elect Tony) were not guaranteed a long electoral shelf-life.

While his Dáil career was comparatively short, Sherwin achieved more longterm success at City Council level. He served nineteen years as a councillor. In fact, Tony and he were to overlap in their membership of the City Council for two years. At the time of his death in 1981, Sherwin was chairman of the Council's inner-city committee. While Sherwin lacked Tony's firmer political compass, he was a colourful figure who inspired much affection. One of his trademarks was his bow tie, a curious foreshadowing of Tony's distinctive rejection of any tie in the attire of his political persona!

Sherwin was 'old style' but the remaining five Independent council-lors elected in 1974 were more 'new style' – Independents elected for the first time and standing under the Community Independent banner. This term was a new flag of convenience politically, a very loose form of iden-tity which created some distance for the candidates from traditional party loyalties. The implication of the title was that these candidates claimed a primary commitment to the communities that elected them rather than to any political party whip. Two of the five elected had strong environmental-ist credentials: Carmencita Hederman, who was identified strongly with planning and architectural heritage issues in the city, and Sean D Dublin Bay Loftus, whose strong focus for a considerable time had been the pro-tection of Dublin Bay from being spoiled by industrial development.

Of the five, the one whose path would cross most with Tony's was Kevin Byrne from East Wall. Byrne was elected as an Alderman (a distinction accorded the first elected in the area) to the City Council in June 1974 on a 'Community Independent' ticket. He was a social science graduate, and also a qualified secondary teacher. He claimed to be 'four generations an East Waller'.[21] He took a range of stances on diverse issues in his five years as Councillor. Tony also used the Community Independent label when his turn came to stand for elected office, but this did not mean that Tony and Kevin Byrne had a closely aligned 'take' on key issues. They shared a common con-cern about local industry and environmental safety, and a scepticism about official responses, but on other fronts their views could diverge, notably on a row that blew up over a Combat Poverty project for the north inner city.

In 1976, the NCCC had succeeded, almost, in securing agreement with

Combat Poverty – a government appointed body with a brief to support anti-poverty initiatives – on a grant for a local project in the inner city hosted by NCCC and the North Centre City Community Action Project (NCCCAP). Kevin Byrne intervened in the process late in the day, objecting to the lack of involvement by city councillors in the project – such involvement would, of course, open the door to his participation, a case, it would seem, of his trying to cover his political back. In the end, the project proceeded, but not before Tony sent a letter to *The Irish Times* in which he issued a stinging rebuke to Byrne for what Tony saw as his interference.[22] Tony accused him of seeking to claim credit for the project, when actually he had had no involvement until he started complaining:

> **Mr Byrne apparently believes that he can use his political weight to 'muscle in' on what is essentially the achievement of the NCCC. If that be the case, then, Mr Byrne is very much mistaken.**

But even with an emerging base of community projects and committees, there was still no guarantee that the ordinary local resident or tenant would get a generous or even a reasonable hearing from the powers that be. The following quote reflects the experience of one woman decanted to Foley Street from the notorious Corporation Buildings in Corporation Street in the north inner city in 1972. Six years later the corporation were back to extract her from Foley Street, the next block on the list of the demolition squad. But the woman in question was not playing according to the script. She had had enough of moving when the Corporation was in the mood. Here's an account written by a community activist:[23]

> **My own mother was shifted around to Foley Street [in 1972]. But she swore she would never move again for the Corporation. But the time came – the Corporation came in then and they decided they were going to knock Foley Street down then – this was the eighties. So my mother said she wasn't going to move, and she stuck to her guns. So what took place then was they re-housed every tenant out of Foley Street but she**

wouldn't go … at the end of the day she was the last there, and they were demolishing the place around her, and they cut off the electricity, they cut off water, they created leaks in the roof and the whole lot … at the end she had to give in – her health just got the better of her.

But ultimately the lesson was that local resistance to official plans would not always be successful.

Reflecting on his decision to stand for election to the City Council in 1979, Tony claimed that he could do much better than any of the existing crop of councillors at representing the interests of local residents and communities. Looking at the approach of previous local Independents such as Kevin Byrne and Frank Sherwin, it was clear that Tony would represent a real changing of the guard, quite apart from clear differences he would have with the approach of the mainstream political parties.

It became clear to me that the local councillors were totally out of touch with anything that was going on in the north inner city. It absolutely amazed me that any of them could have been elected. I mean we had to go and seek out these people, we had to go and find out who the hell they were! … what I'm saying is that it seemed self evident to me that we as a community group would have no difficulty getting someone elected. I was absolutely convinced. There's no way I would consider standing if I didn't think I was going to get elected, I just couldn't see the point of that. So I stood and I was elected to the City Council in 1979.[24]

Even on his first electoral outing, Tony was wise enough to know that actually getting elected required a huge amount of hard work. The first campaign made up in enthusiasm what it lacked in experience or resources. Canvassers were dispatched often without enough leaflets to serve the batch of addresses they had been allocated on the day. One canvasser recalls being sent out without enough leaflets, and the advice from his organiser was to release the leaflets only to those people who seemed to hold promise as possible voters! The situation on that particular canvas that evening was eventually rescued when Noel arrived on his bicycle mid-canvass clutching a new batch of leaflets that the printer had just delivered for free.

The scarcity of leaflets might have been a problem, but there was no stinting in the effort to deliver a clear message well. Michael Harnett was a supporter with a public relations and marketing background and a connection through his involvement in the Dublin Tutorial Group. He applied his know-how to help Tony achieve a very high-quality design in his leaflets. He also influenced an impressive decision: to vary in subtle ways the editorial content according to the local priority issues in sub-districts of the electoral area. Certainly for the time, and even for today, this was sophisticated stuff, especially for an Independent standing for the first time. In his first campaign, Tony also had a well-designed poster using a photograph specially taken at Tony's request by Derek Speirs, a well-known photographer in both current affairs and social documentary work – his work was frequently used by *Magill* magazine, at the time a very successful and ground-breaking monthly current affairs magazine with a strong instinct for social justice. Again, the use of Derek Speirs's work was further evidence of the professionalism that Tony was bringing, even as a novice, to his electoral efforts.

Election day came and went and the count that followed would reveal whether Tony's optimism was justified. The overall count went on long into the night, and gradually over the successive counts intrinsic to the process of proportional representation, it became clear that Tony would, indeed, win a seat. In some counts, there is high drama as fortunes wax and wane over various counts and margins remain very tight. In this instance, it was more of a case of low drama – joy, but no drama. The favourable trend emerged reasonably early in proceedings, even if Tony had to wait a long time for the formal declaration. Tony won his Council seat with a combination of enough first preferences and a healthy supply of later preferences from other candidates – a 'formula' that would stand him in good stead in later national elections.

CHAPTER 3

• • • • • •

From the Council
to the Dáil

In his first election campaign in 1979, Tony had tasted success. He had won a seat on Dublin City Council. It was a huge achievement and one that meant a great deal to his team of supporters. For many of them who had supped too long at the cup of exclusion, the symbolism of Tony's success was enormous. It was a moment and a status to be savoured – the election of Councillor Tony Gregory.

Tony was one of five Community or non-party candidates elected out of 45 councillors in total. These five were: Sean D Dublin Bay Loftus (non-party, Electoral Area 1); Johanna Barlow (Community, Electoral Area 3); Tony Gregory (Community, Electoral Area 6); Carmencita Hederman (Non-Party, Electoral Area 10); Brendan Lynch (Community, Electoral Area 11). The other four had been re-elected, having stood successfully for the first time in the 1974 elections.

Electoral success meant that Tony was suddenly plunged into close engagement with Dublin Corporation officials – the senior staff of the Council, who implement the policies of the Council and play an influential role in helping to shape and formulate such policies. They are the 'civil servants' of the Council. In principle, they implement policy as laid down in broad terms by the councillors. In practice, as with the civil service, the Council officials are very influential not just in interpreting or applying policy, but also in formulating it. They exert a lot of influence because typically they have more of the critical specialist knowledge on a given issue than many councillors may have. But with Tony it would be a different story. He had the commitment and the ability to get to grips with critical issues in sufficient depth. As Tony took office as a councillor, the reality he faced was that the officials serving him as a councillor were the same ones whose approach he had bitterly opposed from outside the tent – he had resolutely fought them on issues such as housing develop- ment and the planning of motorways.

It is safe to say that the relatively cosy relationship that typically existed between elected members of the Council and Council officials did not apply in Tony's case. Indeed, one insider from the early days can recall Tony and a senior official shouting abuse at each other – only half in jest – on the staircase in the Council offices.[1] It must have been quite a rude awakening for officials to have their conventional way of operating challenged – and more especially to have a critic who had done his homework. The year before his election to the City Council, a picket by Tony and other inner- city activists on the city officials' Christmas party was one example of how these 'troublemakers' from the inner city drove home their point.[2] Mick Rafferty remembers a poster they used on that picket which was designed to aggravate then Assistant City Manager Davy Byrne, the person they saw as one of their main opponents in the management team of the City Coun- cil. The poster boldly proclaimed, with cheeky humour, that 'Davy fiddles while the inner city burns', shamelessly filching the lines about Emperor Nero and the destruction of Rome.

But it was one thing to be outside the tent, hurling in criticism, it was quite another to suddenly find himself on the inside, and it proved quite a challenge, as Tony describes, although it didn't mean that he changed his views:

In the tenants' organisation we spent most of our time attacking the Cor- poration, occupying their offices etc. The danger is when you become a councillor, you become part of that and see them as nice people doing

**their job. But once in the job they seem to become people with no sensi-
tivity to an area like this, no understanding of it, and no interest in it. They
will see a thing like a park, and a lake, as being a great achievement in an
area of the most abysmal poverty that you could come across. That as a
demonstration of the bureaucratic mind is classic.**[3]

There were many points of conflict with Council officials, some that
had blown up in advance of Tony's election. There was the issue of a 'housing needs assessment' sent by the Council into the Department of the
Environment without adequate scrutiny by councillors, according to Tony
and some of his fellow activists. There was the decision of the Council,
announced in August 1978, to demolish tenements in Summerhill, Gardiner Street and Sean McDermott Street without, in Tony's oft-repeated
view, adequate consultation with the local residents. It seems difficult to
exaggerate the gulf in attitude between the activists and the officials. In
November 1979 Fergus McCabe served three days for a protest blocking
traffic at the Gardiner Street/Summerhill junction six months earlier; he
had refused to be bound to the peace at a hearing of the case because he
wished to reserve his right to continue to protest for a cause he considered
just. The protest was in relation to Dublin Corporation's plans for housing
in the area. Fergus vividly recalls a 'consultation' meeting where the Corporation officials met community representatives to listen to their views
on re-development plans for the inner city. A Mr Ryan was the Chairman
of the Summerhill Residents Association; he ran a small business, a shop
that sold baby clothes on Summerhill, where he lived over the shop. He
was a very gentle man and certainly not one to make his contribution in
any offensive way. Fergus still remembers Mr Ryan being 'put in his box'
by an official when he tried to make a point at the meeting. The message
clearly was to 'sit down and shut up.' The story illustrates how, within the
Council management, a culture of non-accountability to local concerns
and views had become embedded. This was undoubtedly linked to low

voter turn-out and low voter registration in the area. All of these issues – accountability, voting and registration – became issues that Tony tackled head-on.

Another issue on which Tony resolutely resisted Council policy was on the proposed Eastern Bypass motorway from Whitehall to Merrion Gates, which was in the sights of planners in the late seventies and early eighties. He was implacably opposed to the construction of such a motorway. With his characteristic force and clarity, he set out the case against it in a piece in the monthly paper *Hibernia* in 1980. He argued that the intended route had already caused planning blight, that its construction would destroy at least 150 houses on its route, and that its elevation on stilts in parts would aggravate the risk of pollution.[4]

In September 1979 the north inner city came close to having the eyes of the world cast upon it, months after Tony's election as a councillor, when Church and State joined together in a remarkable show of coordinated efficiency to put a rare gloss on the city for the visit of Pope John Paul II, the first pope to visit what was still at that point a staunchly Catholic country. In this context, the inner city area got some attention. Like the proud housekeeper readying the house for the visit of the relatives so as not to let the family down, the Council set to work and many obscure corners received a lick of paint, mostly in the papal colours of saffron and white. These colours were to remain in place for many years after, not out of any special respect to the memory of the pontiff's visit, but more as a true reflection of the normal rhythm of redecoration when papal visits were not on the agenda. One memory of this author's is the painting of the boundary railings in St Joseph's Mansions on Killarney Street on the off-chance that the papal cavalcade might pass that way out of deference to Matt Talbot, the nearest thing to a saint that the inner city could claim (he had been a local man reputed to wear chains in reparation for his previous excesses with alcohol). Some of the more hopeful locals had convinced themselves that the pontiff would drop in to the local church in Sean McDermott Street, but they were to be disappointed. The papal cortège drove past without stopping because it was behind schedule. The 'papal visit that wasn't' seemed another apt symbol of the area's marginalisation, this time by the Church rather than the State. But in the anti-climax, the locals had the consolation of presentable railings in papal shades, even if the rest of their complex still cried out for attention. However, the Jesuit Peter McVerry recalls with some bitterness that the reality was even bleaker than I realised:

He [John Paul II] was to stop off in the church on Sean McDermott Street but was behind schedule, and he passed us by on the way to meet the bishops and dignitaries in Dublin Castle. That really pissed me off. The other thing that pissed me off was when the Corpo painted the railings and walls on Mary's Mansions [on Sean McDermott Street] for the visit – but only on the two sides that the pope would see.[5]

Change did not come quickly in terms of any new approach to planning and development in the inner-city area. Just over two years after his election as a councillor, Tony was still bitterly critical of the Corporation strategy. In an interview with Fergus Brogan in *The Irish Times*, he is quoted as saying:

If the Corporation had any imagination or understanding, they would have had a phased development, and demolished and rebuilt gradually, and retained the community, but they regarded it as something rotten in the heart of the city and wanted it taken out.[6]

This issue of the official attitudes inside the Corporation ran very deep. Tony, as councillor, recalled what he saw as the miserable mind-set of Corporation officials in the case of Liberty House, a run-down flats complex off Sean McDermott Street (note the irony of the title under which residents had to labour):

Liberty House was built in 1940; they are tiny little flats with not even the most basic facilities of a bath or a shower in them. The tenants there

got the idea that as you could not build baths on to them you could provide shower units in them at a fairly small cost. The first response of the
Corporation was that they did not have the money. But it was pointed out
to them that they did have the money in that area because they had sold
a site to the Department of Education for a million quid and they were
using this million quid to build their park that would bring prestige to the
Corporation, but had nothing to do with the local people.

Prior to the general election, when City Councillors will support anything,
we pushed through this thing that every tenant in Liberty House would
get a new shower unit. But at the first meeting of the City Council since
the election the officials took the almost unprecedented step of objecting
to the showers. So here we had the Assistant City Manager objecting to a
thing like showers in Liberty House, which ranks much lower than Sheriff
Street; it's possibly the worst-off urban community in the country.[7]

But the problems, in Tony's view, were not just to do with the attitude of
key officials, he was also bitterly critical of the senior politicians who represented the inner city in the Dáil and who, in his view, had failed to deliver
the major change it required. In the piece in *Hibernia*, he did not hold back.
Despite being represented by George Colley and Michael O'Leary, among
others, and despite their skills and status as being among 'the country's leading politicians', Tony argued that the inner city lay trapped in policy neglect:

... neither, during their years in power, ever introduced any initiative to
meet the needs of the most deprived urban community in Ireland today.
The leading establishment politicians are apparently content with occa-
sional appearances in the inner city rather than any concerted effort to
achieve radical changes. The poverty that exists today is to a large degree
the legacy of their political failure ...[8]

Neither Colley nor O'Leary lived in the constituency, and Tony's criticism of both of them seemed to hit the spot in terms of how distant they
were, in many senses, from their constituents. Colley's mode of campaigning

in the area included laying on free rounds of alcoholic drink in certain bars there, indicating a lack of real political engagement with his constituency. Tellingly, Tony did not hold back in critiquing the failures of the Left also:

> **… nor has the Left attempted to fill this political vacuum. In disarray as always, and troubled only by their own ideological differences, the Left has not responded to any significant degree to this issue on what one would have thought all left-wing groups could have shared a common platform.[9]**

With such negative views of the local TDs, it must have seemed very tempting to Tony to take them on in a Dáil election, especially after his success in the Council election. Initially, Mick and Fergus were sceptical of the idea of Tony pursuing their shared political agenda through the route of representative democracy at national level. As far as they were concerned, having elected representatives had not served the inner city well: the inner city had entered into unchallenged terminal decay and neglect on the watch of representative democracy and the politicians it had thrown up. Having either low-profile local politicians or high-profile national politicians as its representatives had made no difference to the fate of the area. There was no evidence that the incumbents or the system could deliver the change that was required. Tony, on the other hand, seemed to have long harboured the idea of standing for election. In this, he was undoubtedly influenced by the example of how, in Wicklow, Seamus Costello had used his work as a local politician to advance the causes he believed in. Costello had also wanted to stand for the Dáil in the 1969 election in Wicklow, but he could not get support for this break with the long-established Sinn Féin principle of abstentionism from parliaments implicated in Irish partition. Taking seats in such parliaments, in their view, lent legitimacy to partition, therefore abstentionism was the only correct response. Looking back on his own decision to stand for the Dáil, Tony explained, in a radio interview on RTÉ with John Bowman, that 'I wanted to be a full time political activist.' Such a level of commitment and engagement was necessary, he felt, for 'a worthwhile contribution'.

As Tony considered his political prospects for election to the Dáil from the vantage point of his local Dáil constituency, and of his smaller more local City Council electoral area, the results from the 1973 and 1977 Dáil elections and the 1974 Council elections might have given him certain tentative clues as to the instincts of the local electorate. As might be expected, given relentless national trends at the time, the dominant force in 1973 was Fianna Fáil, which won two seats with George Colley and Celia Lynch. Colley was a Fianna Fáil heavyweight and a defeated leadership contender when Jack Lynch won the leadership in 1966 and when Charles Haughey won it in 1979. The party hoovered up 42.3 percent of first-preference votes with its three candidates. What might be regarded as the broad Left mustered four candidates – three for Labour and one for Sinn Féin – and gained 25.8 percent of the vote, yielding a seat for Michael O'Leary. In the 1977 election, the constituency was reduced from four to three seats. The broad Left, with three candidates, achieved 29.1 percent of the first-preference vote – an increase on 1973 of 3.3 percentage points. The gain was achieved by Labour, whereas Sinn Féin's share actually declined, of which more later. Fianna Fáil still dominated, this time with a 41.1 percent share of first preferences. A new ingredient in the mix was the emergence of a Community Independent from East Wall – Kevin Byrne, who had come from the ranks of the City Council.

From Tony's perspective as a potential Left-leaning Community Dáil candidate, there were two interesting points. Firstly, there was the emergence of Kevin Byrne. East Wall lay east of the North Strand between the city centre and Fairview, within the Dáil constituency that would be Tony's target for winning a seat. On his first outing in the Council elections in 1974, Byrne had topped the poll in Dublin Area 5, the other councillors elected there being Michael Keating and Ray Fay (both Fine Gael), Tom Stafford (Fianna Fáil) and William Cumiskey (Labour). In the 1977 Dáil election, Kevin Byrne won 1,913 first-preference votes (8 percent of the vote). Byrne was articulate, but was possibly higher on self-importance than doorstep appeal. But his two performances in the Council and Dáil elections certainly indicated a niche in the electoral support that might lie waiting to be tapped by another Community candidate.

Secondly, Sinn Féin The Workers Party (SFWP) had changed candidates between the two elections and had lost ground in terms of actual first-preference votes gained. In a spectacular own goal, SFWP had contrived to dump Máirín de Burca, one of their best-known figures nationally. She had a strong national profile, thanks to her identification with many causes of the oppressed and her typically feisty and articulate performance before any microphone, television camera or journalist's notebook. She had won 1,667 (4.8 percent) first-preference votes in the local constituency, then entitled Dublin North Central, in the 1973 general election. This was a respectable performance for a first outing, both in absolute vote numbers and in percentage terms. It was easily the best performance of any SFWP candidate in that election. The vote she achieved also suggested that she had the potential to build this voter support over time into a decent electoral base with the prospect eventually of winning a seat. But the secretive and powerful 'Industrial Department' of the party thought otherwise. Led by Eamon Smullen and Eoghan Harris, the Industrial Department decided it would be more appropriate to have a mainstream trade unionist standing for the 1977 election, and they chose Ray McGran, a young candidate with a strong background in trade union and trades council activity. In the event, the new candidate did less well, winning only 1,138 votes, a drop of just over 500 on what Máirín had achieved previously, thus squandering the momentum generated by her performance in 1973.

Recalling this decision to 'lose' de Burca as the candidate, former SFWP activist Pádraig Yeates comments that

basically they shafted her with the nomination thing and put forward Ray McGran, who on paper fitted their criteria perfectly; he was young, recently married, he was a very active member of his own union, he was president of the trades council ... he did very poorly, but Máirín was totally shattered by that experience, you know, because they just took her out, basically, and she left [the party] shortly afterwards.

Clearly, de Burca was seen as a loose cannon, too independent-minded for those who pulled the political strings in SFWP. Having the status and experience of having served as co-secretary of Sinn Féin at one point did not prove sufficient protection; neither did being a founder member of the Irish Women's Movement, nor being co-founder of the Dublin Housing Action Committee. But in the cynical calculation of Harris and Smullen, 'the homeless did not vote' as Pádraig Yeates puts it. Being popular with the homeless, or defending their interests, did not bring in any votes.

Actually, an unintended consequence of Máirín de Burca's 'disappearance' as a candidate was that it cleared the way for Tony more easily to stand. In Pádraig Yeates's view, Tony would not have stood against her, partly out of respect for her activist role and also out of personal loyalty based on their time together in Sinn Féin. His reluctance to stand against her would additionally have been based on a fear of splitting a potential common vote between them. It was a delicious irony of the situation that Harris and Smullen were actually, in a sense, instrumental in launching Tony Gregory's political career. It was an irony that Tony must have savoured, given that he and Harris took different positions on many issues.

Mick Rafferty concedes that, in advance of Tony's electoral successes, he (Mick) under-estimated the power of the mandate and therefore the negotiating clout that winning a seat gave – that was especially true in negotiating with State bodies, whose stock attempt to disarm community representatives had always been to ask: 'Who precisely do you represent?' In one sense, it was a reasonable question, but it was also a dead hand on the lever of potential change. It was a kind of political 'snooker' that local activists could not easily escape, no matter how strong the objective facts of their cause or case. Being elected transformed this imbalance. An elected politician had a mandate to ask the questions and make the demands, a mandate that had to be respected by those running the machine of public administration.

TONY'S FIRST GENERAL ELECTION 1981

Having weighed up the evidence, Tony decided to make his first bid for a Dáil seat in the 1981 general election. Dublin Central – his local constituency – was a five-seater. Whatever his camp may have lacked in collective experience, they certainly made up for in enthusiasm and effort, as well as in Tony's efficient organisation. In the final analysis, it was Tony's call whether to stand, but he gained the full support of his camp. While it had been blooded in a preliminary way in the Council elections in 1979, his machine was still a novice organisation in many senses, but also one with an amazing ability to produce the goods – quite literally in some cases. There were all kinds of unexpected resources and connections that would be revealed on election day. At the time of this first Dáil election, each candidate worth their salt had to ensure they had a presence at each polling booth throughout election day to harass or cajole voters as they made their way into the building, usually a school, where the polling booth was located. The assumption was that voters were undecided as they made their way into the polling station and a vigorous assertion of a particular candidate's case would be the decisive final influence. This was all nonsense, of course, and such late bombarding of voters was eventually banned. But at the time, no serious candidate could afford to step back and grant the competition free rein, so everyone was trapped in the same game. Being able to play this game was no mean feat, logistically. It necessitated ten to twelve hours' cover across countless sites in the constituency.

Achieving this level of cover often meant long shifts, especially in the early part of the day. One activist in Tony's camp was heavily pregnant on her first outing on duty at a polling booth in Glasnevin – Mary Quinn, this author's wife. But she recalls being the recipient of a lot of kindness from opposing teams and from the officiating Gardaí, who were present to ensure the general security of proceedings. Mary was offered a chair and the odd sandwich, with no hint of antagonism as to her auspices. Ironically, the Gregory machine was able to outperform the other parties and candidates in terms of support to their polling booth activists – a salad lunch, delivered by van. This was supplemented by tea and nibbles supplied by a local newsagent sympathetic to Tony's cause! The Gregory camp was also able to muster transport from their ranks to ensure that less mobile or less motivated voters were delivered to the polling booth. In this, the Gregory organisers were fast learners – they were merely imitating the experts, following how Fianna Fáil and other political high achievers had done things over the years. The back-up within the Gregory camp certainly seemed a lot better than the support systems available to SFWP.

Though he wasn't elected, Tony polled 3,151 first preferences, a very respectable result for a first outing in a Dáil election. This result was certainly a strong endorsement of the decision to stand and an encouragement to work to improve the performance at the next election, due normally, according to the Constitution, in not more than five years. Tony had gained 6.8 percent of the vote, meaning he had come seventh in first preferences, ahead of Luke Belton (Fine Gael) who was the third Fine Gael candidate, Pat Carroll (Labour), Micheal White (SFWP) and Jimmy Somers (Labour). The five seats went in order of election to Bertie Ahern (Fianna Fáil), Michael Keating (Fine Gael), George Colley (Fianna Fáil), Michael O'Leary (Labour) and Alice Glenn (Fine Gael). This was also Bertie Ahern's first outing, and he topped the poll, a feat he would continue to achieve over many subsequent elections. Significantly, Ahern had outperformed the long-standing Fianna Fáil TD for the area and national figure George Colley. In what was to prove of special significance ultimately, there was a dramatic drop in the share of votes achieved by Labour Party Leader Michael O'Leary; in the previous election in 1977 he had gained 20 percent of the vote, but this time his share had slipped to 10 percent.

There was a quiet satisfaction and confidence in the Gregory camp. They might not have won, first time out, as they had in the Council election in 1979, but everyone knew that a Dáil election was a much bigger undertaking – a bigger area to cover with tougher competition. But they felt they were on track, and with effort and determination they would eventually reap their just reward. One possible glitch was that Tony had achieved a slightly smaller share of the first-preference vote than had Community candidate Kevin Byrne in the previous election in 1977. But this was a marginal difference and not one that registered strongly with the camp; the bigger issue was to watch the fate of Michael O'Leary and his share of votes. The votes he lost had to go somewhere.

The result reinforced certain realities. In the bigger constituencies for the Dáil, compared to the smaller wards in Council elections, Tony could not rely solely on his hardcore of inner-city supporters to elect him. There just weren't enough of them, especially when you subtracted those who voted for the other parties, those who didn't vote and those who were not even registered to vote. In the inner city, voter turn-out and voter registration were low, posing a special challenge for those relying on that area as their electoral base. Tony tried to address these problems, but, overall, the implication was clear: he had to gain votes from *all* parts of the constituency, even from voters living in the leafier and slightly 'posher' neighbourhoods – all or parts of Drumcondra, Glasnevin, Marino, Cabra. Tony quickly realised the importance of communicating regularly with these voters through local and national media. He proved no slouch in self-publicity: from this moment on, every possible opportunity for his name to appear in print or on television or radio was grabbed. And clearly the strategy worked.

The style of electioneering in the Gregory camp was consolidated in this first Dáil election and carried forward to the two elections in 1982 and future campaigns. Tony was deeply hands-on in the business of election-eering. The evening canvass would be organised with military precision. The team would assemble in Sackville Gardens, get their supplies of leaf-lets, directions to their zone of operation, and some words of advice and encouragement. They would then head for the front doors they had been allocated. There was a natural limit to enthusiasm: it would be imprudent to knock on a door after the 9 o'clock news; at the very least, it might be counter-productive. After the canvassers drifted home or went to the pub, their evening's work done, Tony would set out in a van, driven by Pat Carthy, to put posters on lampposts from eleven o'clock right up to two o'clock in the morning. Widespread postering was used during campaigns to assert a high profile across the constituency, and Tony did not shirk from the hard physical work that that involved. His trick in postering was to make sure his poster was the highest on the lamppost. This was more hazardous for the person doing the postering, but better for the candidate, whose poster would be less subject to interference by mean-spirited opponents. Pat Carthy's job was to drive, and to hold the ladder steady. One night during the first 1982 Dáil campaign, Tony and Pat were down in the East Wall area, Pat's home territory, postering away outside a school. Tony was up the ladder negotiating the challenge of securing the poster to the lamp-post, Pat was below, holding it. Pat smoked a pipe at the time, and feeling the urge for a puff, he sneaked away for a moment to grab his lighter from the van. Unfortunately, Tony shifted his position on the ladder at the same moment and it keeled over with Tony on board. 'Could you not ★★★★ing concentrate for a few more minutes?' was Tony's understandably cranky rebuke as he dusted himself off. Undeterred, Tony kept on postering, saying he was fine despite the mishap. The next day, Pat discovered that Tony had actually gone to the Accident and Emergency unit in one of the local hospitals around four o'clock in the morning, long after they had packed in the postering for the night. It turned out that Tony had broken his wrist, leading him to sport a plaster of Paris covering throughout the first 1982 election campaign. Indeed, the same plaster of Paris can be spotted by the eagle-eyed in photos of the Gregory Deal negotiations in Summerhill Parade a short time later. The story underlines two recurring features of Tony's approach – his unquenchable appetite for hard work, and his strong sense of privacy. Lesser mortals might have dragged Pat off to A&E, but partly pure Tony, partly Irish male, Tony wanted no fuss made about medical matters, even for something as mundane as a damaged wrist.

ELECTED – 1982

Tony had two election campaigns behind him. He had won a Council seat in the first and performed credibly on the larger stage of a Dáil election in his second electoral outing. Dáil elections normally come around every four to five years or so, a cycle based on the constitutional requirements. So Tony could expect to have a good interval in which to consolidate his positive showing in his first Dáil election and build a stronger support base that would deliver him a seat second time round. But in many ways politics is the art of managing the unexpected, as Tony was to discover some eight months later. Governments are elected and defeated inside the Dáil on the basis of the overall votes of the deputies who have been elected by the people. Barring accidents, most governments expect to serve their full term, relying on the stable majority that has elected them. But in the 1981 election, a minority government led by Garret FitzGerald was elected which depended for its establishment and survival on support from other deputies, beyond the Fine Gael/Labour governing parties, who were willing to give support. This meant the government had to be careful to keep its support-ers, and especially its 'external' supporters on board. Retaining these key 'external' votes involved vigilance in spotting issues that might cause trouble among supporters, thus jeopardising the working majority the government had engineered.

The minority government was up and running, everything was going smoothly, and the annual budget for 1982, to be introduced by Finance Minister John Bruton, was expected to be voted through in the normal way. But then, suddenly, the minority government contrived its own defeat by failing to spot that introducing VAT on children's shoes in the budget would scare off key supporters – and so it proved. The government was defeated on a budget vote, by its own naivete and lack of vigilance, and an election had to be called.

Suddenly a new chance to be elected had opened up for Tony, much earlier than expected. It was a chance he grabbed with both hands as he geared up his election machine for yet another round of postering, leafleting and knocking on doors, this time in the cold, dark month of February. The motivation of his team was sky-high despite the dreary weather conditions. Tony and Noel marshalled the eager troops each evening as they came to collect leaflets for delivery to the different estates and flats complexes in the constituency.

As the votes were counted it became clear that Tony had won a seat. There was great jubilation, and his talent too was being noticed. In a profile of Tony on his election, Frank Kilfeather, local government correspondent for *The Irish Times*, wrote:

> I have seen Gregory come through the political nursery of the City Coun-cil. For one so young, he shows an incredible political maturity. He pos-sesses an amazingly quick political mind. He is highly articulate. He can express his case with clinical brevity and lethal effect. It is done in a quietly

effective manner. He never rambles, and does not like to see others waffling. Time is too important to be wasted.

Frank Kilfeather, The Irish Times, *24 February 1982*

His election was indeed a huge cause for joy and celebration for all in the Gregory camp. But though there may have been great reason to party, as the story unfolded it turned out that Tony and his close associates would have little time for partying.

Above: Tony Gregory with his beloved mother, Ellen, and their dog, Rex, and cat, Maggie, in the early sixties. The photo was taken in the back garden of their house at Sackville Gardens. (*Source: Gregory family*)

Right: Tony's parents, Anthony and Ellen, on their wedding day, 1944, with the extended family. (*Source: Gregory family*)

Left: Noel Gregory (left) on his First Communion day with his brother, Tony, and their father, Anthony, May 1952. They are at Dublin Zoo as a First Communion treat, and the photo was taken by the boys' mother. (*Source: Gregory family*)

Below: Sackville Gardens, along by the Royal Canal near Croke Park, home of the Gregory family. (*Source: Pat Langan*)

Left: Noel and Tony visiting Santa outside McBirney's, Dublin, *circa* 1954. The boys were taken to a different department-store Santa each year. (*Source: Gregory family*)

Right: Tony, aged seven, at Dublin Zoo on his First Communion day, 7 May 1955. (*Source: Gregory family*)

Above: Tony and Noel on their holidays at their mother's family's place in County Offaly.
(*Source: Gregory family*)

Opposite, above: Tony Gregory, second row, third from left, on his Confirmation day, with his class from St Canice's national school, 1958. (*Source: Gregory family*)

Below: Tony Gregory, front row, second from left, with his classmates at O'Connell's secondary school, Richmond Street, Dublin 1, in the mid-1960s. Tony won a Corporation scholarship to attend second-level education. (*Source: Gregory family*)

UNION OF STUDENTS IN IRELAND
ASSOCIATE MEMBERSHIP CARD

PHOTO

Surname
GREGORY

Forename
ANTHONY

NO.
8503

Nationality:
IRISH

Signature:
Anthony Gregory

Educ./Estab.:
University College Dublin/
Graduate

Issuer/Org.:
Union of Students in Ireland

Date 27.4.1973

Signature of Issuer:
Mary McCabe

Opposite: Graduation from UCD in 1969 with a BA degree.

Tony obtained a Higher Diploma in Education the following year.

Insert: His travel card from the Union of Students of Ireland in the 1970s. Graduates could avail of travel concessions with this card.

(*Source: Gregory family*)

Right: Tony observing the knocking down of tenement slums in the north inner city in the early 1980s.

He campaigned for proper housing for the people he represented as a city councillor and later as a TD.

Below: Tony taking part in an anti-internment protest in 1971.

A youthful Tony – with attitude! – 23 April 1985. (*Source: Derek Speirs*)

● ● ● ● ● ●

CHAPTER 4

Negotiating the Deal

W hen the dust settled on the election results on the evening of Friday, 19 February 1982, it suddenly became clear that Tony could play a pivotal role in the election of the next government. The Community Independent candidate from Dublin's north inner city had won a Dáil seat at his second attempt. Tony Gregory had displaced Fine Gael's Alice Glenn, who was a colourful and socially conservative Fine Gaeler with a gift for getting publicity: in the divorce referendum in 1986, she was to say that 'A woman voting for divorce was like a turkey voting for Christmas.' Tony had won the fourth seat in the five-seater constituency, ahead of Michael O'Leary, the Labour Party leader – quite a coup for a relatively novice candidate. Tony had won 4,703 first preferences, a few hundred less than O'Leary, but had gradually overhauled O'Leary thanks to successive redistributions of later preference votes under the proportional representation system. Bertie Ahern (Fianna Fáil), Michael Keating (Fine Gael) and George Colley (Fianna Fáil) had won the other seats, in that order.

As the results came in, the numbers began to stack up in such a way, nationally, that neither Fianna Fáil on its own, nor Fine Gael and Labour together, would have a majority – they would each need other votes beyond their own members in the Dáil to elect their nominee for Taoiseach and to form a government. The first hint of the potential of Tony's new status as a key supporter of whoever was to form a government came from Albert Reynolds, then a senior figure in Fianna Fáil, and a later Taoiseach. In a television interview on election night, as he assessed the implications of the results, Reynolds said that he expected that the newly elected Tony Gregory would support Fianna Fáil. As Colm Tóibín put it in a piece in *In Dublin*, which he edited at the time, 'without warning, the door opened'.[1] It was a remarkable turn of events for a candidate whose campaign nerve centre was the front room in the family home from where Tony and Noel directed operations, as compared to the former State Cinema in Phibsboro which, as Noel Gregory recalls, local Fianna Fáil candidate Bertie Ahern had used for his campaign. The family home down at the end of the short cul-de-sac that was Sackville Gardens, along the Royal Canal, served as central storage for election materials as well as the check-in point for all activists. It was like stepping back in time entering the room on the right of the hallway – Election Central. It belonged to another era, rich in the colours and memorabilia of past times, in the style of Tony and Noel's parents. The team also had the use of the NCCCAP offices at 20 Summerhill Parade, a few sparsely furnished rooms they used occasionally for meetings during the election campaign.

The extraordinary outcome, that Tony could hold the balance of power in the formation of a new government, led to much activity in the days that followed. The three main party leaders – Fianna Fáil, Fine Gael and Labour – all asked for meetings with Tony but, as it turned out, with different degrees of conviction and urgency. The Gregory camp prepared a two-page document to present to them, setting out the issues on which Tony had been elected. As Tony saw it, the three big issues were unemployment, housing and educational provision.[2]

Fianna Fáil were first off the blocks, having sent the initial signal through Reynolds's comment on television on the night of the count. In the lead-up to the negotiations, Charles Haughey, the Fianna Fáil leader, wanted Tony to visit him in his mansion in Kinsealy, County Dublin, but Tony insisted that all meetings had to take place in the modest offices at Summerhill Parade.

And so it was to be. Both sides had access to advice from the City Council on some of the costings and estimates affecting some of the proposals. Haughey relied on his brother Seán, who was Assistant City Manager, and on Fianna Fáil members on the Council. Tony, a councillor himself, could call on Frank Feeley, the City Manager, and on senior officials for briefing on the costs for his various project ideas.

Garret FitzGerald, outgoing Taoiseach and leader of Fine Gael, also came to Summerhill, where he had one meeting with the Gregory camp. Garret had written on personal notepaper to Tony on Friday, 26 February, exactly a week after the election results, and three days after Haughey had actually met the Gregory people. In the short note, Garret said that 'my party has authorized me to have discussions with you' and asked Tony to call his office to set up a meeting.[3] When they did get to meet, FitzGerald brought with him Jim Mitchell – to act as his 'interpreter', as Tony put it later. Because of his origins in the south inner city, Mitchell was a rare animal in the Fine Gael landscape, a high-profile politician with serious electoral appeal in working-class areas, not the natural source of Fine Gael votes – Fine Gael, historically, was the party of the middle classes and the big farmers. FitzGerald, then still Taoiseach pending the instalment of the new government, and Mitchell were met on Saturday, 6 March, by Tony and Noel Gregory, Fergus McCabe, Mick Rafferty and Philip Boyd. Fergus recalls Mitchell smoking Hamlet cigars during the meeting, a quirky detail that stood out against the spartan setting. This was the first opportunity for Fine Gael to make a response to the two-page document from the Gregory side and the meeting was taking place three days before the due date for the election of the new Taoiseach. The timing, so close to the deadline, hinted that neither side was wholehearted in their engagement.

Despite being a local TD and leader of the Labour Party, Michael O'Leary could not see his way to venturing deep into the darkest heart of his own constituency, as far as Summerhill Parade. O'Leary had proposed a meeting with all the left-wing TDs outside Labour: Limerick TD Jim Kemmy of the Democratic Socialist Party; the three SFWP TDs – Proinsias de Rossa, Paddy Gallagher and Joe Sherlock – and Tony Gregory. He suggested they meet in the Dáil. For various reasons that meeting did not materialise. In the event, Tony and Noel met Michael O'Leary in Wynn's Hotel. O'Leary was very downbeat about his ambitions or prospects in terms of the shape of the next government. Perhaps realistically, he was basically saying, 'There is nothing I can do for ye.' The *realpolitik* was that the electoral numbers meant that O'Leary was not going to be elected Taoiseach. But, as it turned out anyway, O'Leary's heart wasn't in it in more ways than one – months later he was to resign the leadership of the Labour Party in order to join Fine Gael, quite a remarkable changing of political horses. Tony's position throughout the process was always to declare support for a 'Left alliance in the Dáil', but negotiating this proved elusive in practice.

Reflecting on the process of Tony negotiating with two aspiring Taoisigh, the then Fine Gael politician and UCD law professor John Kelly reportedly observed, with his characteristic wit, that here was a case of 'a tail wagging two dogs', which is certainly how it must have seemed to many observers.[4] But it was not easy being that tail doing the wagging.

The door may have opened, as Colm Tóibín put it, when the election results came in and made Tony a potential king-maker in the appointment of the Taoiseach on his first day in the Dáil. Yet, making the most of this scenario would test the skills of even the most seasoned politician, not to mention a neophyte. He had been dealt the cards, but could Tony play the hand?

Tony had no immediate template to follow, no 'heavy' political experience to draw on. Instinctively, he knew he faced formidable opponents and that he should aim to avoid giving any advantage to his adversaries. They would have to *negotiate*. By insisting on meeting Charles Haughey in the spartan conditions of his office at Summerhill Parade rather than in the luxurious surroundings of Haughey's home in Kinsealy, at least he would have home advantage. He insisted his key advisers would be present – there would be strength in numbers, and he would need the support of his close allies to authenticate and sell the terms of any deal that might emerge. His followers would have to trust the process. Tony was also well prepared – true Tony – he had a document ready to present to Haughey at their first meeting; not the final set of demands, but an outline of the scope of his concerns. Tony also showed skill in managing the process on his own side.

On the one hand, the negotiating scenario was impossibly imbalanced. Haughey, the most experienced, the most wily, the most determined politician was up against a complete novice. But, on the other hand, there was an exquisite simplicity and symmetry about the situation – Charles J Haughey needed a vote and Tony had it. But, however you looked at it, it really was a case of David versus Goliath, certainly in the case of Tony negotiating with Haughey, and even with FitzGerald, or indeed O'Leary.

Tony was a novice TD, aged thirty-three. Charlie was aged fifty-seven, and vastly experienced politically. He already had eighteen months as Taoiseach under his belt in the period 1979-81. He had been leader of Fianna Fáil for just over two years, he had been a TD for twenty-five years, and had eleven years of experience in ministerial office. He also had one year's experience as a Dublin city councillor (1954-5). Tony could draw only on three years as a city councillor.

Even with Garret FitzGerald, there was a clear imbalance. Garret was fifty-six and had chalked up seven months as Taoiseach before his government imploded. He also could draw on the experience of thirteen years as a TD, four of those as Minister for Foreign Affairs.

Haughey was not hanging about. The Gregory camp had the first of four meetings with him on Tuesday, 23 February, four days after the election results. The Gregory team gave Haughey their two-page outline position and they got a forty-page document back from him on the following Wednesday week.[5] The final discussions took place on Sunday, 7 March, with Mick, Fergus, Noel and Tony present.[6] They also met FitzGerald that weekend. At both meetings that weekend – with FitzGerald and Haughey – Alan Lund of the *Northside News* was granted access to take photographs.

When setting up the meetings, Tony had said to Haughey, 'I'll have four or five people with me', to which Haughey responded: 'That's fine – you can have as many as you like. I'll have nobody with me.'[7] Haughey was dropped off at the offices by Bertie Ahern. Meeting the Gregory team on his own demonstrated Haughey's great self-confidence. It was hard to know what was crossing his mind as he climbed the dimly lit and rickety staircase that led to the poky venue – Camp Gregory, a set of small rooms upstairs that passed as their offices. Looking back on this first encounter, Fergus McCabe reckons that 'it was quite brave of Haughey' to venture into the unknown in this way.

While the negotiating team knew their man, not every local person would actually recognise him. Fergus recalls an amusing incident in the lead-up to the Deal that captures this. Joe Kershaw was a local young person, now sadly deceased, who was heavily involved at the time in some of the youth projects supported by Tony and his team. He happened to be in the building when Haughey arrived on one of his visits. Sensing this was someone important, Joe posed the reasonable question, 'Who the f*** is that?' in his characteristically blunt style, and on being told, Joe was heard to mutter the immortal words: 'F***in' Haughey!'.

As he sat down at the table for what was to be the first round of discussions, Haughey said, 'Right, lads, you know what I want, now tell me what do you want?' In the second meeting, Haughey said he could go 'more than half way' on most things on their shopping list – 'You're pushing an open door' was a phrase he liked to use in his contact with the group. But there was one exception. 'Lads, for jaysus sake, I can't nationalise the f***ing banks!' – he was responding to an opening gambit in the Gregory initial document. He also baulked at the idea of star trade unionist Phil Flynn, of the Local Government and Public Services Union, being chair of the proposed Inner City Authority. In those days before the Peace Process in Northern Ireland, appointing a Vice President of Sinn Féin to such a position was a bridge too far. Haughey also declined Noel's radical job creation proposal to help reverse job losses in the docks – to build an oil refinery in Dublin Bay, that Noel argued could be financed with Russian money – Noel had tried the idea out on Charlie as they walked down the stairs after one of the meetings. An earlier attempt to promote an oil refinery in Dublin Bay in the early 1970s by Acquarius Securities Ltd, with the support of the Dublin Port and Docks Board, had failed (see Chapter 2), thanks in part to the efforts of Sean D Dublin Bay Loftus, who ran highly successful political and electoral campaigns against threats to the ecology and integrity of Dublin Bay. In late 1981, ever-vigilant Dublin Bay Loftus claimed that the Dublin Port and Docks Board was seeking to revive the idea. The idea Noel tried out on Haughey was in the air, even if the suggested source of funding might have represented a radical departure for the Irish authorities. And nobody would dispute that investment for jobs was badly needed at the time, and a state-owned refinery with Russian support might have been more palatable politically than a private company owning it. But, clearly, Haughey didn't bite. At the time, this author was working for the national office of the Society of St Vincent de Paul and I had a strong focus on policy issues to do with the needs of older people. I already knew Fergus, Mick and Tony, and they knew slightly of this policy work. During the Deal negotiations Fergus phoned me to ask for my input on those issues to the Deal document. My main suggestion was the idea of free medical cards for those aged seventy-five and older – an element that got into the final Deal. Apart from its value to the beneficiaries, this provision was an example of how the terms of the Deal were not always parochial.

On a number of fronts, this one included, the impact reached far beyond the north inner city.

A few years later, Tony recalled the atmosphere and approach in the Deal process:

> Every single thing in the Deal was something which the community in this area had at some stage decided was an objective worth obtaining. There were a few exceptions – things like closing the Curragh Military Prison. People would come to us and say, 'Will you ask for this?' and we were sympathetic, so we just included it. But the major things had come forward from the people in this area and nobody else ...

> I remember having a meeting of local people in two rooms in Summerhill Parade while the discussions were going on. I said to them I had deliberately asked three people to be there any time I met with Haughey or FitzGerald so that they would know there was nothing underhand and that anything we were looking for would be something we had all been fighting for for ages. So it satisfied all the local people, all who had been involved in my canvass and electioneering. So people now feel that, for example, the housing scheme in Seville Place is something that I got. It wouldn't be there if we hadn't fixed it a couple of years ago. You know, that's very important. Fr Duggan said at the AGM [of the local community association in Sheriff Street] that the people had shown it was possible to get something which they thought was impossible. And that's the perception people here had. People from middle class areas reckoned I was being bribed by Haughey. I don't know how many phone calls I got from people asking me about the house he had bought me in Howth and so on.[8]

Pressures of the negotiations themselves led to huge demands from the media and other groups that Tony could never have imagined or prepared for. As Fergus recalls:

> As it became clear some sort of deal was on the cards, Tony and the rest of us began to get representations from various groups and individuals – some imploring Tony not to vote for Haughey, others the opposite ... It

was an unbelievably hectic time – especially for Tony who as well as being engaged with all the meetings and policy formation processes was practically hounded day and night by the media. But it was also hectic for all of us, the most engaged community activists in the Gregory group who were also working in our own jobs as well. Tony, of course, was under the most extreme pressure. He said at the time, and afterwards when reflecting on the Deal period, that the media attention was the most stressful aspect of the whole experience. It is hard to overestimate the amount of media interest and coverage and that for a guy who was a political unknown. The name recognition engendered probably gave him political credit for the rest of his career, but with the non-stop pressure and little sleep it must have taken a huge physical and psychological effort to keep going at the pace he did during the deal period. He was lucky too that he was not a real drinker in any sense of the term as he would have been unable to do what he did if he was.

When the process was more or less completed, Haughey was desperate to confirm that he did actually have a Deal that would translate into a vote to support his election as Taoiseach. The negotiators in the Gregory camp were playing it cool, suggesting that he would have to wait until the day of the vote to find out. But Haughey, the wily old fox, caught them on the hop with an appeal to the emotional heart strings: 'Ah lads, if I am going to be Taoiseach, I would like to have my wife, Maureen, and children there …'. Softies that they were, they gave in and confirmed that Tony would vote for him on the basis of the agreement. As they parted for the last time in the process, Haughey said to the Gregory team, 'As Al Capone once said, it was good doing business with you.' Reflecting on the process years later, Tony observed:

Haughey's real achievement in these negotiations was that he succeeded in winning over the support of the inner-city activists involved with me. He had started off as the rank outsider, the untouchable as far as they were concerned, and yet he managed to end up as the unanimous choice of all of my group.

Looking back, Fergus recalls that the tone of the meetings and the body language of the visitors to Summerhill Parade pointed towards Haughey being more capable of delivery. He was closer to the numbers to make a deal work. Garret was offering less and the electoral numbers had fallen less in his favour. In the case of the negotiations with Haughey, both sides knew they didn't like each other, but each had something the other needed – the perfect basis for a deal. It was 'strictly business', Fergus observes.

The underlying attitudes of the two leaders towards the Gregory team proved very important, as Mick Rafferty underlined. In the case of Haughey:

We wanted him to understand the implications of the document from a social point of view. We tried to describe to him what it meant to be homeless and deprived. We felt that he understood. He wasn't looking for a vote for Taoiseach; he *was* Taoiseach.[10]

There was a different atmosphere, Mick recalled, in the contact with FitzGerald, who seemed to misjudge the situation:

He reminded me of a schoolteacher. He didn't want to listen. He had bits of paper in his hand; without any blackboard chalk, he was lost. We weren't there to be educated. We were there to be listened to.[11]

Nuala Fennell, a Fine Gael politician of the time, conceded, in retrospect, that FitzGerald was 'half-hearted' in his negotiations, wary as he was of committing to greater public spending in the context of what he saw as the dire national finances.[12]

While discussions were held with three potential taoisigh, in practice there were only two who were realistic prospects – Haughey and FitzGerald were the ones with anything close to the numbers needed to be elected. Given Tony's republican background, it was unlikely that he could easily embrace a deal with a Fine Gael leader, whose party historically was hostile to a republican analysis on the Northern question. The *realpolitik* of the situation was that FitzGerald did not belong, politically, to the extended republican 'gene pool' to which Tony could relate. Tony's associates, Fergus and Mick, might, on the other hand, have had to swallow hard at the prospect of a deal with Charlie Haughey; Fergus and Mick were more comfortable with FitzGerald's line on the North and his broadly social democratic instincts. But in fact, developments played into Tony's hands. Garret proved to be too far removed from the reality of the north inner city, politically and socially, to 'get' where the Gregory camp was coming from. FitzGerald proved much too tentative in his approach to discussions. He was much less specific, and too vague, in what he would promise. Mick recalls that Garret came back with proposals that were seen as being too 'abstract'. A piece Garret wrote years later in *The Irish Times* also revealed the ambivalence he had felt about negotiating deals with Independents. Haughey, on the other hand, could lay claim to being a Dubliner in his carefully composite range of origins, including roots in counties Derry and Mayo. He happily presented himself as a northside boy with a natural – or skilfully cultivated – affinity with the working class Dub. However far he rose up the political or social ladder, he never forgot his roots, or so he liked people to think. His long political experience also meant that he was likely to have the skills to massage political solutions that advanced his interests. Haughey entered wholeheartedly into the process of identifying and articulating policy responses that engaged with the concerns of the Gregory camp. He instructed Martin Mansergh in Fianna Fáil Head Office to do his homework in advance on Gregory's likely logic and priorities.[13] His brother Seán, as Assistant City Manager, helped to put flesh – and costings – on many of the initial ideas. Overall, Haughey brought a much more 'can do' spirit to proceedings, while Garret tended to have a more '*ochón, ochón*' spirit, emphasising the gloomy prospects facing the country – he mostly spent his time trying to convince the Gregory team of the reasons things could not be done. His vision for change seemed to them much more timid and less impressive.

At the last of the meetings with Haughey in Summerhill Parade, when things were clearly going well, Mick suggested that they should mark progress with a drink. 'Taoiseach, would you like to have a drink in the Sunset before you go home?' he asked. He noticed that Haughey clearly liked the form of address, even if it was still a little premature – his long-time opponent, FitzGerald, still actually held the office. When they came outside, it was raining, so they chose to go next door to Belton's rather than to the bar Mick had suggested, Sunset House, on the corner of Summerhill and the North Circular Road that was farther away. Belton's was then part of a famous chain of Dublin pubs, owned, as luck would have it, by Paddy Belton, a true blue (northside) Fine Gaeler! They arrived in the pub – then 'a kip' in Fergus's recollection, certainly not up to the standard that the man with a taste for Charvet shirts might expect. Drinks were ordered – pints for the lads and a more refined gin and tonic for Charlie. As the barman told them the total for the round, Charlie explained that he didn't carry cash! – that was clearly for lesser mortals. Mick likewise had no money on him, not that he had any principled objection to carrying cash. Tony did not rush forward to offer and Fergus recalls that he was the one who 'blinked first'. Charlie couldn't resist a spot of teasing: 'Lads, would ye never think of joining Fianna Fáil?' at which they smirked into their pints.

ANNOUNCING THE DEAL

On Tuesday, 9 March, the day the Deal was to be made public and the Dáil was to reconvene after the election to vote in the Taoiseach, Tony and Philip Boyd were in the team's offices in Summerhill Parade. In their hands they had the final version of the Deal, complete with the vital signature of Charles J Haughey. The signing by both sides had been witnessed, the night before, by Mickey Mullen, General Secretary of the Irish Transport and General Workers' Union, truly an iconic union in Irish labour history.[14] Mullen had been asked to witness the deal by the Gregory side, not by

Haughey as some media sources surmised at the time: the Gregory people already had contact with Mullen through a catering course for local unemployed young people that he had facilitated being run in Liberty Hall. The media had wrongly assumed that Haughey had used his union connections to line up Mullen. Noel had met Mullen after the election and Mullen had offered to be of help in any way he could.

Word had leaked out the previous day that a deal was on the cards between Haughey and Tony. SFWP-leaning University College Cork history professor John A Murphy expressed his disapproval in characteristically colourful terms, and got in a dig at Haughey's wealth; its source was always an Achilles' heel politically for Haughey in those times, and indeed later became the focus of a tribunal of inquiry in which he was held to have acted corruptly. Murphy commented acidly:

There is an element of farce in the sight of a millionaire island owner seeking to woo a representative of the poorest people in Dublin.[15]

That morning Tony went home briefly from the Summerhill office before heading for Leinster House for the beginning of proceedings, leaving Philip Boyd in charge of getting the document to the media. It was an exciting moment, but there was a problem. Philip found himself with just one copy of the thirty-page Deal, typed, signed and ready to go, but he was short a photocopier. The humble resources of the office in Summerhill Parade did not stretch to a copier capable of producing copies of a document that size in the numbers required. Clutching the copy of the Deal to his bosom for dear life, Philip contemplated his next move as he descended the stairs, where he was instantly door-stepped by the journalist Stephen O'Byrnes (a few years later to become General Secretary of the Progressive Democrats), who had shrewdly been hovering outside in expectation of some action. 'What's happening?' O'Byrnes demanded. Thinking quickly, Philip waved the document in O'Byrnes's face and exclaimed, 'This document will elect the next government.' O'Byrnes rather predictably asked, 'Can I have a copy?', to which Philip, more creatively, responded, 'You can have the first one, if you pay for a taxi to get me to a photocopier.' They went to Philip's work-place – he worked as an engineering draughtsman in the Department of Post and Telegraphs offices then in Cumberland House in Fenian Street. In slightly unparliamentary language, Philip's boss asked where he had been, as Philip had been AWOL for a few days, caught up in the heady business of deal-making. A strong Haughey supporter, his boss mellowed considerably when he heard what Philip had actually been up to and what he had in his hand – the key to Haughey being elected Taoiseach. The boss cleared the photocopying room, locked the door and ensured that the desired number of copies materialised in double-quick time. The impromptu press officer for the Gregory camp then set off on foot on the short journey to the Dáil, where he distributed copies to the assembled hacks. The well-known Derry journalist and left-wing activist Eamon McCann was among them and as he scanned the detail of the Deal, he expressed admiration to Philip for what had been secured: 'This is great stuff.' (See Appendix 1 for full text of the Deal.)

Tony embraced the 'young student look' as he crossed the plinth at Leinster House to enter the Dáil chamber for the first time on the fateful day when he traded his vote for the Deal. Smart casual, it might have been, but, despite the strict dress code about ties in the Dáil, there was no tie – a point of great interest to the media. He wore a sports jacket with jumper. Somehow, nobody tried to hold Tony to account for this departure from convention and his trademark lack of tie was never to be breached in all his later time in the Dáil. Tony was accompanied to the Dáil by Noel, Fergus and Mick, all modelling an array of jackets , jumpers and a lone duffle coat – *fashionistas* on tour. Noel, as family, had a special place in the visitors' gallery. He looked down proudly on proceedings, still pinching himself at what had been achieved. Ironically, the carefully crafted Deal nearly came unstuck because the three SFWP deputies, unfamiliar with the geography of the Dáil chamber had managed to get themselves locked out of the '*Tá*' (Yes) zone for the election of Taoiseach. A quick-thinking Fianna Fáil backbencher, Mark Killilea, spotted the problem and physically hauled them across a barrier to rescue the situation. Tony's efforts had nearly come to nought!

TONY'S MAIDEN DÁIL SPEECH, ANNOUNCING HIS SUPPORT FOR HAUGHEY[16]

Since my election to the Dáil my advisers and I have had extensive talks with Deputy FitzGerald, Deputy Haughey, Deputy O'Leary and the other Independent groups. At all these meetings we presented the contenders with the same basic proposals. These proposals were exact and specific developments of the issues for which I stood in the election.

Two major considerations dictated our approach to these negotiations: first, to try to get clear commitments from a future Taoiseach on tackling the issues with which we are concerned and on which I was elected; secondly, we were conscious of the responsibilities placed upon us to interpret the balance of political forces in the Dáil and to make a decision that would encourage the development of progressive and class politics. This was no easy task.

I interpreted the result of the election and my own election in particular as demonstrating that the two main political parties have failed to respond to the needs of our society. I had no illusions about the differences between the main political parties. Policies, not personalities, influenced my decision. The decision I have come to has not been taken lightly and certainly not with a view to maintaining any particular party in power. My decision is purely tactical and based on achieving as many as possible of the issues that I was elected on.

Specifically, my decision is based on a clear difference in response from Deputy Haughey and Deputy FitzGerald. Given the commitment by Deputy Haughey, witnessed and signed by the General Secretary of the Irish Transport and General Workers' Union I had no alternative but to support a Fianna Fáil Taoiseach. The issues to which Deputy Haughey committed himself included a major increase in Dublin Corporation's housing programme, which has been a scandal for years, the allocation of £91 million for housing in 1982, and a commitment to reach 2,000 houses by 1984 was given. Four hundred new houses in the north centre city area will be started this year.

Mr E Collins: What about the rest of the country?

(Interruptions.)

An Ceann Comhairle, John F O'Connell: This is Deputy Gregory's maiden speech and it is customary for no interruptions to take place during a Member's maiden speech.

Mr Gregory, Independent: I regret, though I understand it, that some members of the Opposition do not appreciate the importance of these commitments. I certainly do. I should like to go on with the details and the basis on which I shall give my support to Deputy Haughey as Taoiseach. An almost total breakdown of Dublin Corporation services will now be averted as a result of a commitment by the Leader of Fianna Fáil to allocate a further £20 million to Dublin Corporation's budget for this year.

On the issues of employment we put specific proposals to Deputy Haughey. He committed himself to an immediate work force of 500 men costing £4 million for a corporation environmental works scheme and more than 150 additional craftsmen at a cost of £1,500,000 in addition to the present staff to be employed and to give a major boost to the corporation's repairs and maintenance service. A commitment to nationalise Clondalkin Paper Mills to save the jobs of 500 men if no other option presented itself immediately was given. This commitment is a demonstration of a new departure and attitude to the development of our natural resources.

The controversial and destructive motorway plan will not now be proceeded with. The vital 27 acres on the Port and Docks Board site will be nationalised and developed along lines geared to the needs of centre city communities. In the field of education a major commitment to pre-school education along with the provision of a £3 million community school for the neglected centre city area was given, this being part of the designation of the central city area as an educational priority area. Advances in the taxing of derelict sites, office developments, financial institutions and development land were agreed to. A national community development agency will be set up for a budget of £2 million to replace and continue the work of the Combat Poverty Committee.

These are some of a very comprehensive list of agreed policies between my advisers and the Leader of the Fianna Fáil Party. Deputy FitzGerald in his response, though sincere and genuine, was most pessimistic and did not approximate remotely to the commitments given by Fianna Fáil.

(Interruptions.)

Mr Gregory, Independent: Having assessed the responses of the two contenders there were two further considerations which we felt were important.

A deputy: What about Cork?

Mr Gregory, Independent: One was the role of the five Independent Socialist Deputies and the hope that they could agree to a common strategy in electing a Taoiseach. The decision of Sinn Féin The Workers Party not to participate in an alliance prior to the election of the Taoiseach and on the election of the Taoiseach, a decision which we respect as their right, made our hoped-for alliance impossible. The position of the Labour Party was also important to us because of the common ground between us on social and economic issues. Their decision not to participate in Government effectively ruled out any other option but to give conditional support to the election of a Fianna Fáil Taoiseach. Once a Government have been elected they will receive my support only in so far as they pursue the programme of agreed commitments and other acceptable policies to me.

Beidh mé ag votáil mar sin ar san an Teachta Ó hEochaidh sa toghachán le haghaidh an Taoisigh.

In his opening speech as Taoiseach a short while later, Haughey made reference obliquely to the Deal and the commitments therein, and hinted at their wider significance:

We also intend to treat as a major priority one of the areas most affected by high unemployment, the inner city of Dublin. The revival of the inner city of our national capital is in the interests of the whole nation. Our aim is to recreate a Dublin of which the nation can be proud, and to provide an imaginative approach to a problem which exists in many other countries.

Our success in dealing with these problems will be a headline for similar areas in every part of the country.

SAVOURING THE MOMENT

What do you do of an evening after your single vote has determined who is in government? For the first part of the evening, Tony had a date in RTÉ to do an interview on the current affairs programme, *Today Tonight* after the main evening news. Philip was with Tony and after the interview, they took a taxi back to Gregory country for a few quiet pints in Tony's favourite watering hole, Gaffney's pub in Fairview.

Sipping their pints, Tony and Philip must have been a little shell-shocked at what had been achieved by their small group of activists. They had arrived. Tie or no tie, the world had paid attention to Tony Gregory, this articulate and forceful new Dublin voice in national politics. In his profile of Tony in advance of the negotiations, *Irish Times* journalist Frank Kilfeather had also observed, with not a little prescience, that 'Mr Haughey and Dr FitzGerald should not underestimate him when they meet him. They will quickly find they are dealing with a new-style Irish politician.' In his tribute in the Dáil after Tony's death, Labour Party leader Eamon Gilmore, in a similar vein, commented on Tony's skill in exploiting the opportunity that the electoral arithmetic had once given him:

> He showed remarkable political acumen in using the pivotal position in which he found himself in the aftermath of the 1982 general election to highlight the need of his constituents and the broader political constituency he served, and in demanding action to deal with their problems. I am sure all the taoisigh in waiting at that time thought they would have no difficulty in dealing with a political novice but, instead, they found themselves outwitted, outfoxed and out-negotiated.[17]

Writer and lawyer, Ronan Sheehan had contributed ideas to the process of drafting the Deal. When the details broke in the media, as Tony read the content into the Dáil record, Ronan decided he would try to get a flavour of the reaction on the ground:

> I headed for town to savour the atmosphere. I bumped into Mick Rafferty on Summerhill. An old man, grinning form ear to ear, wandered or tottered out of the doorway of O'Neill's pub and shook Mick's hand. 'We didn't take the shilling,' Mick cried. 'We took fifty million.' 'Look at the prizes you won!' the old man said. 'I prefer to call them concessions,' Mick replied. 'I still call them prizes,' said the old man. The little offices in Summerhill Parade were in ecstatic mood. People from the flats around kept calling in to share the atmosphere of triumph. They didn't go into the detail much but sat with huge smiles on their faces, smoking, drinking cups of tea, walking on air when they walked.[18]

POLITICAL REACTION TO THE DEAL

In the Dáil speeches that day, praise for the Deal and Tony came from an unlikely source, from Fine Gael TD for Laois–Offaly and 'Father of the

House', Oliver J Flanagan, the longest serving Deputy. He had a reputation for conservative views, but here he was generous in his sense of the importance of what was at stake:

> **Deputy Gregory referred to the problems of the inner city of Dublin. One would imagine that Dublin belonged only to the people of Dublin. Dublin is our city and we all share it. It is the capital of Ireland. We love our capital, those of us who have not had the privilege of having been bred, born or reared there. We look on it with pride and joy and delight. It is the place to which we come from the country to do important business. Dublin is not the property of the people of Dublin but of Ireland and its people. That is why we are glad to see that some steps will be taken to restore the city to what it was. The city of Dublin has been allowed to vanish before our eyes. I hope that as a result of the united efforts of Deputy Gregory and of all Dublin Deputies of all parties – the Lord Mayor has an important part which I am sure he will play in this matter – Dublin will be built up and that instead of huge office blocks, many of them foreign-financed and foreign-owned, we will have houses and homes so that Dublin people will be able to enjoy living in their own city.**

> **Do not allow foreign office block owners to take over the whole city and drive Dublin people into the country. Dublin people respect and love their city; build it up for them and make it a place where they can live with their flats, their homes, their schools and other educational facilities and not have it as a huge block of aluminium and glass. Let there be children running around and life in the city and do not have many parts of it used for only six or eight hours a day. I am glad that some steps have been taken in that regard.[19]**

It is quite possible that Flanagan had two agendas in his speech – genuinely to welcome the initiative and to get up the nose of Garrett FitzGerald. The two had often crossed swords inside the same political party as liberal versus conservative. Flanagan may have been saying 'Well done, Tony' on the surface, but 'You blew it, Garret' underneath.

There were happy campers in the Deal tent – Tony, Haughey, Fianna Fáilers, and the unexpected visitor from across the political divide, Oliver J Flanagan. But not everyone was so delighted. There were at least some political sour grapes, as in this comment by Gay Mitchell, brother of Jim Mitchell who had accompanied Garret to Summerhill Parade. Mitchell was, as he notes here, a city councillor like Tony. He was also the politician who years later was dubbed 'the evil of two lessers' in the wonderful phrase of Michael McDowell, co-founder and one-time leader of the Progressive Democrats, when baiting the Mitchell brothers.

Having heard the maiden speech of a Deputy from this city, I very much regret announcements which usurp the authority of Dublin Corporation, of which I am a member. The powers of local authorities have already been significantly usurped and I appeal to the incoming Minister for the Environment to implement necessary local government reforms, especially in the Dublin region. Each member of Dublin Corporation represents the same number of people as an average county council. This is a problem which should not be lightly treated. I protest very strongly that a Deputy in his maiden speech should be permitted to say what will or will not happen in the Dublin region when that decision should be a matter for the local authority. I urge the Minister to consider local government reform at an early date.[20]

Gay Mitchell resisted pointing out that Tony himself was also a city councillor in Dublin, a fact no doubt that added salt to Mitchell's wound. In a debate on the budget some time later, opposition finance spokesman for Fine Gael, John Bruton, also took a swipe at the Deal on much the same grounds. He did not, however, address why the institutions he was defending had failed to engage with the festering problems the Deal was seeking to address:

I regret also that a number of items in this budget, although good in themselves – and they are not matters I should wish to criticise on their merits – such as matters concerning the inner city were introduced into

this budget, not as a result of consultations with the responsible authorities such as the health boards, or the corporation, or other local authorities to whom this House delegates responsibility for policy-making, but as a result of conversations between one Deputy and another. That by-passes proper local authority channels. We have local authorities such as Dublin Corporation, and we have health boards such as the Eastern Health Board, whose job it is to decide priorities within their own area of competence, priorities in the matters of roads, education, vocational education committees and social services.

To by-pass the local authority structure – local authorities we established in this House to make policies and to allocate budgets within their own areas – is demoralising and in a sense short-circuits proper democratic processes. I do not believe it is good practice for deals of that sort to be implemented in this way. It is far more appropriate that all the people involved on those local authorities should be consulted. They were elected by the public to decide on priorities and they should have the opportunity to decide what should be done within broad allocations given to them by the Government.

I do not believe policy should be made in the name of this House by two Deputies out of the total number in this House. No deal made between them should become a policy which overrides the proper processes which have been established for the making of policy through local authorities such as the health boards and Dublin Corporation. That is not a satisfactory way in which to proceed, and I very much regret it.[21]

While conceding the benefits that would flow to the north inner city, as a Deputy representing the south inner city Gay Mitchell claimed in a further speech that there was discrimination implicit in the agreement between Tony and Haughey. This time, his tone was a little mellower and less ungracious. And, to be fair, he was raising an important issue, although also, to be fair, there were many points in the Deal document that reached in their impact well beyond the north inner city.

The north inner city will certainly benefit greatly by the deal negotiated between Deputy Gregory and the Taoiseach. In all honesty, I cannot criticise Deputy Gregory too much. All members are concerned about their own constituencies, but one must ask: is finance to be allocated on a regional basis and, if so, is it done on an economic basis? In Dublin an allocation has not been made to the south Dublin inner city which is equally as deprived. That area suffers enormous unemployment, has very bad housing, ugly sites and many other disadvantages. I have represented the area for the last seven months, but those issues were raised by many of my predecessors and they did not meet with any great success. Suddenly huge sums of money are made available for the north inner city. In my view that form of financial discrimination is questionable and I do not feel there is any objectivity in those proposals contained in a signed and witnessed document ... The money for Dublin Corporation is very welcome. However, the way in which it came about is regrettable. There is no question of objectivity about it. Any attempt by the Minister to continue to interfere with the autonomy of Dublin Corporation will be resisted by this side of the House. The Minister has already caused the roadway proposals made by the Fianna Fáil group in the City Council to be reversed in one fell swoop. This is because of the voting situation in this House.[22]

Charles Haughey, in his contribution to the budget debate, sought to set the commitment reflected in the Gregory Deal in a wider context of concern for urban disadvantage generally, in a speech that undoubtedly had ambition, but also some bravado — and a distinct flavour of fudge:

To match our commitment to regional development, we are at the same time undertaking a comprehensive new programme of urban renewal. It has become increasingly clear in the last decade that the regulatory powers of the planning Acts are not sufficient to bring about the balanced economic and social development needed to create living neighbourhoods in our inner urban areas.

We have decided, therefore, to intervene in a positive and energetic way to regenerate those inner urban areas which have suffered economic, social and environmental decline and decay through a combination of unbalanced investment and neglect. Our approach is threefold. We will set up by legislation, which will be introduced almost immediately, development commissions for areas of particular neglect in any of our towns and cities. There will also be an inner city authority for Dublin in the first instance to implement economic, social and educational measures for the whole inner city area. Also local authorities are being provided with funds for programmes of special relevance to inner city areas.

We are initiating this programme in the Dublin city area but our intention is to extend it to other similar areas in other towns and cities. Already some elements of our programme have been extended to areas outside Dublin, like our £1 million fund for the rehabilitation of dwellings in the inner city areas.

Our commitment to intervening by a combination of administrative, financial and taxation measures to bring back stable neighbourhood life to our inner cities is one that has widespread support throughout the community. We will bring to this programme the same enlightened resolve which in the past cleared the slums and built the great housing estates of the suburbs.

We also intend to improve the quality of life in the suburbs. Too often in the new large housing estates there are instances of social, cultural and economic deprivation even amidst greatly improved housing and neighbourhood conditions. The National Community Development Agency, which will have a fund of £2 million this year, is a new effort to improve the quality and content of community life by combining State aid and the resources in self-help and voluntary effort of communities faced with economic and social deprivation.

Our concern to correct the economic and social inequality between inner city areas and other areas which have benefited from the economic and social progress of recent decades is part of our general concern to reduce economic and social inequality in our society.[23]

Later in the budget debate, Liam T Cosgrave (Fine Gael, Dún Laoghaire) was also critical that the benefits did not flow more equitably:

> As regards the proposals for Dublin's inner-city, while the apparent millions are to be welcomed, perhaps helped along by Deputy Gregory — so far a fairly consistent supporter of the present Government — I would not begrudge the inner city any of this money for housing or house reconstruction or for derelict sites. What I would question as regards spending public money is the equity of spending over the country in general. It should not just be millions for Deputy Gregory in Dublin or for Deputy Blaney in Donegal.[24]

LIFE GOES ON

Outside the Dáil, work proceeded on the implementation of the Deal. The Gregory team had a number of progress review meetings with Charles Haughey. In this author's capacity as a contributor to the Deal (on issues to do with old age), I was invited to one of these review meetings with Haughey. It was held in the Taoiseach's office in Government Buildings – an impressively spacious and tastefully decorated and furnished room. Haughey met us – Tony, Fergus, Mick and myself – on his own. I knew from some earlier dealings I had with him that Haughey was a stickler for time-keeping. If he was to deliver a speech at 11.00am, he would be there sufficiently ahead of time to deliver it at 11.00am. Not the form of many of his fellow ministers of any party. His approach in the meeting was similarly impressive. He revealed an encyclopaedic knowledge of the public service and who did what. It was clear he really did understand how the system was meant to work and which people had which responsibilities. He made a few brief notes with a very fine ballpoint pen. He was relaxed, courteous, super-efficient. There might have been a element of theatre, but overall it all seemed very real. He genuinely was *in command*. He made one or two phone calls in the course of the meeting, as I recall, to seek clarification or to move things along on some front or other. The other memory I have is that he was immaculately turned out in a very sharp suit – in stark contrast, it has to be said, to his visitors, who had a more 'street shabby' rather than 'street chic' look – in the cause, needless to say, of authenticity!

The National Community Development Agency was a short-lived venture under the Deal. To some extent it was Combat Poverty under another name, given that Haughey seemed allergic to the previous agency and, indeed, more generally to continuing ventures started by 'the other crowd', a common political affliction at that time. I remember getting a call from Michael Woods, then Minister for Social Welfare, asking me to serve in the new agency. As part of the Deal there was an understanding that on a number of committees being appointed, Tony could have a say on one position. In this case, Tony had given in my name as one of a number from which the Minister could choose. I recall the initial meeting ended with a rather generous lunch for the committee, both held in the Social Welfare offices in Busáras. My main memory of the lunch, hosted by the Minister, is of a large platter of some kind of dessert being ushered in behind a man playing the bagpipes, much to the great enjoyment of the Minister and the bemusement of his guests.

Tony had other contacts with Haughey along the way – some less formal. Tony regularly took part in the annual sponsored cycle from Dublin to Kilnacrott in aid of the Kilnacrott Project. Just weeks after the Gregory Deal had been signed and the new Fianna Fáil government installed, Tony enlisted his new best friend, Charlie Haughey, as the official 'starter' for the event that year on Saturday, 3 April. The conversation between them that day included discussion of Margaret Thatcher's approach to the Falklands War between Argentina and Britain that had just begun, with Tony asking Haughey his views. 'The days of British gunboat diplomacy are over,' was Haughey's response. However, soon afterwards, diplomatic relations between Ireland and Britain reached a new low as Haughey's government took a strong anti-British line, internationally, at the sinking of the *Belgrano* battleship on 2 May 1982 – the Argentinian ship was torpedoed and sunk by the British outside the exclusion zone the British had laid down, causing the loss of life of 323 sailors.

In July, a few months after Tony's first election, the NCCCAP held an impressively ambitious month-long cultural festival called *Inner City Looking On*. Its timing, soon after the election, happened to give the long-planned event the feel of an extended victory celebration. The inner city 'loves a party' as lead character, Frank Gallagher, in the Channel 4 series *Shameless* might say. And not much excuse is needed.

Croke Park has been the scene of many major concerts over the years, with U2 playing their home town one of the favourite draws. In the days before they could command a full house in Croke Park, U2 cut their teeth in a less salubrious or high-profile venue in the inner city. There is wonderful footage of a youthful U2 playing their hearts out on the roof of the playground building in the Sheriff Street flats complex during the *Inner City Looking On* festival. It is probably safe to assume that this is the only time that U2 performed on such a precarious platform in the whole of their careers! By then, the band had two albums under their belt – *Boy* and *October* – and had extensive touring experience in the US, UK and The Netherlands. Songs they played included '11 O'Clock Tick Tock' and 'An Cat Dubh'. The atmosphere was special, and Bono and the boys were clearly enjoying themselves. Mick Rafferty revelled in his role as Master of Ceremonies for the late-night gig, at one point telling the crowd, 'We've got to keep it a bit quiet, somebody is trying to get a bit of sleep in Number 9!' The Gregory camp had again proved they were skilful at accessing resources – and also that they had a good feel for weaving culture and fun into their efforts at community organising.

THE END OF THE DEAL

The warm after-glow of the Deal success spread through the summer, but the longer colder nights of winter brought with them an unexpected hitch. The Haughey government was voted out of office in November when SFWP withdrew their support. Suddenly, the music stopped. Tony's partner had been pushed off the dance floor. The Haughey government fell and it was election time again after only a few months.

The minority Fianna Fáil government, established on the back of the Deal, ran into difficulties early in its term on two fronts. Heavily dependent on every single vote, it suddenly lost two in October with the death of Dr Bill Lougnane and the hospitalisation of Jim Gibbons, both Fianna Fáil backbenchers. Haughey also brought forward at this time an economic strategy 'The Way Forward', aimed at getting public finances back into some kind of shape. The opposition forced a vote on a motion of confidence in the government. The three SFWP deputies found themselves unable to continue to support a government planning severe cuts in public spending. The further loss of these votes meant the fall of the government. Tony faced a dilemma. How should he vote in this vote of confidence in the government? How much loyalty did he owe Mr Haughey as Taoiseach and co-promoter of the Gregory Deal? Goodbye Charlie was tantamount to Goodnight Deal. Yet his left-wing instincts and impoverished constituency meant he could not line up in support of cuts. He announced his decision and his reasons in a speech in the Dáil. He was abstaining, but he wasn't hiding.

It is my intention to abstain today in this vote of confidence in the Government. There are a number of reasons for this decision. The issue is the Government's social and economic policy, cutbacks in the health services and the indications of more extensive cutbacks outlined in the economic plan. The philosophy of the Government's strategy appears to be that when in recession those who are to be hit most are the poorer sections of the community. That is a philosophy I reject and one in which I could have no

confidence, particularly at a time when the wealthiest sections, property speculators and financial institutions, are reaping enormous profits ...

If my vote were to have been the determining factor today, it would weigh very heavily on me as to whether or not I was taking the right decision. No matter what opposition politicians might say, the various concessions made by Deputy Haughey's Government, particularly in the inner city of Dublin, the most disadvantaged urban area in this country, were worth while and morally essential. If any future Government deliberately winds down those measures they will do so to their own eternal disgrace.

I would never have involved myself in discussions with either Fianna Fáil or Fine Gael but for the enormous moral responsibility placed on me as an elected representative from central Dublin holding the balance of power. I make no apology whatever for my actions. I would do it all over again, and if there is to be an election I will fight it on the basis of my commitment to those on whose behalf I have worked as best I could.[25]

All bets were off on the Deal. But even if the Deal had collapsed in a literal sense, it had actually changed the landscape. People saw the inner city differently, both inside and outside of politics. Many projects survived in one form or another. Tony's daring document had genuinely captured the imagination and shifted mind sets. And many core elements did endure or materialise in time – more housing, no motorways, the new inner city second level school Larkin College, renovation of Council accommodation.

It was back to the lampposts and letter boxes as another general election campaign got under way. The well-oiled Gregory machine cranked into gear again and delivered their candidate safely across the line, winning a seat, the second of many such occasions in the future.

For Tony, the excitement and celebration following the election and the Gregory Deal, and then the drama of the Deal partner losing office, inevitably gave way to the humdrum reality of the day-in-day-out grind that is much of parliamentary politics in Ireland.

PART II

• • • • • •

AN INDEPENDENT

VOICE

• • • • • • • • • •

Tony Gregory had burst suddenly onto the national political scene and instantly become king-maker, helping Charles Haughey form a Fianna Fáil government with minority support in February 1982. This young Dub had driven a hard bargain in the Gregory Deal and won admiration for his achievements from all quarters, even from many natural opponents. But the balloon had burst eight months later: the Haughey-led government suddenly lost power after being forced by Sinn Féin The Workers Party to call an election – and Fianna Fáil were defeated. A Fine Gael–Labour coalition came to power, meaning that many of the commitments in the Deal were now history – they were hardly worth the paper they were written on.

Where did this leave Tony politically? His future was now riddled with questions. The momentum of the Gregory Deal would carry him through to election in December 1982 – he was still a political celebrity – but looking into the longer term, what would the future hold for him? Celebrity may burn brightly but it can also burn out pretty quickly. How would the public react over time? Would Tony gradually lose votes and then his seat – and simply fade from view? Would he try to join a political party like most Independents? Most importantly, after the initial excitement and euphoria of early political success, would his political crew be willing to go on serving on the good ship 'Tony Gregory' in the calmer and drearier seas of everyday politics? Would they have the staying power without a lot of return for all their effort? The humdrum reality of the local TD calls for a lot of patience, and Tony had already grown tired of his first career as a teacher. Having the intelligence, flair and stamina to handle the heady days of the negotiations was one thing, but the question was whether he would have the staying power for the long grind of tedious day-in day-out constituency politics.

As an Independent, it would be very difficult to have any serious influence outside a political party, but this was the challenge faced by Tony

Gregory after the Gregory Deal. Could he be the first independent to have real influence from the back benches? Remaining true to his convictions and principles would be paramount, and really important to him, but he must have known too that many backbenchers before him had been been forced to trim their sails according to the political winds.

In truth, Tony was not easily deflected by any one success or failure. There was a bigger picture: he had a clear political agenda and he aimed to serve it the best way he could. Win or lose, the challenges did not go away. There were issues to be tackled – longterm issues, and issues that came up from time to time. As in the process leading to the Deal, Tony did his utmost to play the hand he was dealt in the best way possible. Yes, he had a long view, but he also took each day as it came, politically. His primary commitment was to Dublin's inner-city issues, and day by day he sought out every opportunity to push these issues with characteristic energy and conviction. But he also took up wider issues about which he felt strongly and where he felt he had something to add. The common denominator across all the issues was Tony's push for justice for the underdog. Soon after first being elected, Tony acknowledged that being inside the tent in political terms brought its own challenges, challenges that had been less obvious to him while he was outside the tent. Yet, over the years, he seemed to be convinced that, whatever its limitations, life inside the tent opened up more opportunities politically than did life outside.

To get a full sense of Tony's political contribution from the outset until his death, it is important to put the Deal to one side and to look also at his commitment and achievements on a range of other fronts. This is not to discount the Deal, but it is to argue that it is by no means the whole story of what Tony achieved. In the coming chapters, we will look at the political issues he embraced over his career and his achievements in relation to those areas. His engagement with issues such as drugs spanned the whole of his political career. Others he took up in his time in the Dáil, or where the opportunity presented itself at constituency or wider levels.

In those years, he was often to show the same hard work, the same vision, the same energy, the same unshakeable commitment to justice, the same remarkable attention to detail, the same capacity to bring his team with him, as he showed in spades in the lead-up to the Deal.

CHAPTER 5

• • • • • •

'Brand Tony'

Looking back over Tony's political career, the Gregory Deal stands out as the high point. But, in fact, there are many other feats that also deserve recognition. Tony won a seat in eight of the nine Dáil elections in which he stood – and even in the one he lost, his first, he did very respectably. He also won a Council seat in every Council election in which he stood, and was the councillor elected with the most votes nationally in the 1991 local elections (among over two thousand councillors).

But perhaps his greatest feat was managing to operate on both the local and the national stages for twenty-seven years as an Independent TD, one of longest-serving Independents ever in the Dáil. The scholarship boy grew up to have a work ethic, ability and sharp grasp of detail that carried the day, not just in his education, but also in politics. His political message remained constant: fair treatment for the inner city and other groups that had long been neglected.

His election strategy remained meticulous through all the years, including thorough canvassing and relentless attention to media opportunities which gave him the potential to reach voters beyond the inner-city flats complexes. It also meant careful minding of 'brand Tony' – not that Tony would ever have used the phrase, but he certainly understood the point. In other words, he remained true to his core principles in everything he did and in everything he said. 'Brand Tony' was deeply identified with the inner city, but his political skill meant he was also quietly hoovering up substantial swathes of votes in the other parts of his constituency.

He won the affection of Dubliners beyond the inner city and across the political spectrum, even from people with quite different political instincts who recognised and respected his fundamental decency and integrity. Even his opponents admired, or, more perhaps, envied, his gutsy articulation of the causes he stood for. And it wasn't just the 'jackeens' – even the 'culchies' grew to have a grudging respect for this Dub with attitude. His political achievements were the Deal, his continuous election success, his various innovations, and his eventual status as a Dublin icon, up there with Ronnie Drew and Noel Purcell.

Another attractive point about Tony was that there was no need to cringe when listening to him hold forth on some point or other. He had a great command of the *two* official languages. His English was characterised by careful expression and proper pronunciation, all bathed in an unmistakeable and reassuringly authentic Dublin twang. His Irish would pass the critical scrutiny of even the most ardent *Gaeilgeoir*.

Being an Independent TD may give certain freedoms, but these come at a price. In an aside in a radio interview with John Bowman, around the time of the vote on his Private Member's Wildlife Bill, he observed that, unlike politicians in political parties, he did not have the 'luxury' of a Whip system. While the Whip restricts freedom and forces party members to vote in the way ordained by the party leadership, it also, in return, gives party politicians 'cover' in relation to many issues. They do not have to make their own decisions in each case and, even more importantly, to justify their viewpoint or their vote. Mainstream politicians can actually hide behind the Whip, avoiding the intellectual effort involved in making up their own mind. But Independents have to make do on their own. Tony, however, was amply equipped for the intellectual demands of assessing every scenario and formulating his response.

On every issue, Tony had to make up his own mind. On every issue, Tony had to face the media and answer their questions. He had to decide what to say every time a microphone was stuck in his face. And he had to do this without the infrastructure of support that party politicians have grown to expect and rely on. He had no media handlers, no programme managers, no researchers in his party offices, no party HQ and no press office filtering demands or issuing instructions and guidance. He could consult supporters, but in the end he had to formulate his response, decide his position, argue his case himself. When there was a speech to be written, a press release to be drafted, it was Tony himself who did the work. He often prepared for interviews or other media outings late into the night. Reading back over his speeches and his articles, and knowing that he was the sole author, underlines his remarkable ability, and I have quoted extensively from his own words in this book, drawing on his speeches, interviews and articles as his own voice gives a strong, unique and contemporaneous feel for Tony, the politician. He had a great gift for expressing his views with clarity and economy and this shines through in all of what he had to say. Tony treated words with great respect – they each had value and were not to be wasted.

The great skill in the delivery of a speech, however, is undoubtedly the ability to make what is fully prepared look 'off the cuff'. Tony's partner in later life, Annette Dolan, says that his speeches and contributions were all honed in advance (see Appendix 2). He took his input into debates seriously and he did his homework in order to achieve the highest quality of content and delivery. He crafted his speeches carefully and delivered them well. Tony quickly grasped the fundamentals of political communication. His message was consistent and he took every opportunity to get it across. He was disciplined and methodical, thorough and highly organised. He paid attention to every detail. Nothing was left to chance. Still, public speaking or addressing a crowd at public events did not necessarily come easily to him; Pat Carthy recalls that even though he was an experienced speaker, he never overcame those nerves just before the performance.

Media coverage was like oxygen for Tony politically. This is true for all politicians, but especially for Independents who lack a party machine and a party brand. The key point about Tony and the media was that he had the skills and capacity to get the most out of any opportunity that presented itself. He had the intelligence and articulacy to respond effectively, to see and make the relevant points. He may have mellowed slightly over the years in how he said what he said, but essentially the message remained the same. And he was always a master at being clear about what he wanted to say.

It helped that he had been a teacher – standing in front of classrooms full of students gradually teaches you to see what works in terms of getting the attention of your audience and getting your points across. It is no accident that politicians have often been teachers – teaching helps to sharpen the skills of communication (and, of course, the work schedule leaves space for politics).

A few on the inside may have known that Tony's command of the media interview was the result of a lot of preparation and apprehension in advance, but in front of a microphone he spoke confidently, always to the point, always in a way that brought conviction and clarity to bear on the issue. He spoke to the question with honesty and economy. Each media performance left people clear where Tony stood and reminded them why they liked his approach. It also re-emphasised how he was different to other politicians who might have been less clear and direct in what they had to say. His approach might be said to have been characterised by the three Cs: clarity, conviction and consistency. Tony was refreshingly direct and 'fudge-free'.

As became clear over his long career, Tony was no parish pump politician. He certainly minded his own political backyard, but he also spoke out on many issues well beyond his constituency remit. His ability to take positions and make speeches on a wide range of issues was remarkable for an Independent.

Another price that an Independent can pay is isolation. They lack the ready camaraderie and solidarity of fellow members of a political party. Just as Tony did not belong to a party, he did not belong to the political establishment either. While many admired his stances, there were others who remained suspicious of his republican roots and sympathies. And even on the Left, rivalry or previous shared history only gave rise to tensions; his former colleagues in Official Sinn Féin generally gave him a very wide berth in Leinster House. Yet being an Independent worked very well for Tony – he had a better chance electorally on the broader-based ticket that being an Independent gave him. He clearly had correctly surmised that belonging to a party from his part of the political spectrum would not have had the same electoral appeal. He had the intellectual ability and the organisational skill to pull off being a successful Independent TD. His strong sense of privacy, and his default position of distrust at many levels, made it better for him to plough a lone furrow. But above all, it was probably his stamina and constancy that won through for him and allowed him to be one of the longest-serving Independents ever, second only to Alfie Byrne.[1] This longevity and consistency is rare among Independents.

Tony brought qualities to the table in his negotiations with Charles Haughey for the Deal that were gradually revealed more widely in later years. One of these was a steely determination. He knew what he wanted, where he was going and he would not be deflected. He knew what he was talking about. He knew the inner city intimately and the other issues he championed. He believed deeply in the main cause he and his associates were advancing – the inner city had long been neglected and where there was a chance to argue its case, Tony grabbed it with both hands. This strong commitment and focus were evident in how he and his close associates handled the Deal process. But an equivalent sense of focus was discernible in how he conducted himself over his whole political career, right up to his final illness and death in 2009.

Many newly elected Independent TD are 'one-hit wonders'. They are elected on one issue but lack the organisational skill, stamina and political 'nous' to dig in and secure re-election. Or they gradually grow weary of the isolation, and gratefully clamber on board the decks of a political party. Constancy is not a feature of some of the more colourful figures on the left. Even the one-time darling of the Left (and a hero of Tony's), Noel Browne, was a member of at least four political parties. Browne had been celebrated for reforms he achieved or attempted as Minister for Health, especially in providing treatment for TB when it was a national scourge, but despite the abiding honour he earned for this work, his subsequent political progress followed a very idiosyncratic path. John Horgan, in his biography of Browne, laments that, over his career, Browne increasingly dissipated his 'passion and ability ... into one organisational cul-de-sac after another'.[2] Tony did not engage in zig-zag politics. He was no political diva. He also was profoundly a democrat. He saw his task as earning the trust of the people and honouring that trust. He set his course, and remained true to his own political coordinates right through his political career. There are not many Independent TDs of whom that can be said. One might be the former Dublin TD, Frank Sherwin, who also served the inner city. He too had an instinctual commitment to the small man, but he did not have the overall philosophical framework that Tony brought to his politics, nor did he achieve the electoral longevity. In addition, Tony had a finely honed political judgement. Ruairi Quinn acknowledges this in his political memoir, when he highlights the fact that Tony had repeatedly said to him, correctly as it transpired, that Bertie Ahern would not call a general election until the last possible moment in 2002.[3]

Tony brought rare qualities to the political table and forged a unique model of community politics. The uniqueness of his ability is further proven in the absence to date of durable copy-cat candidates in similar constituencies across the country. He started his electoral campaigning using the label

'Independent Community Candidate', but over the years this gradually was simplified to 'Independent'. But 'Independent' was not just some flag of convenience, politically, for Tony, some way of signalling that he had no connection with or obligation to any political party: there is ample evidence that Tony actually thought for himself throughout his life. He had ideas and a mind of his own. He was no prisoner to any ideology in an uncritical way.

His friend John Lynch recalls inviting Tony to join him on a guided political tour to Moscow in the days of the Soviet Union, then a union of socialist republics led by the Soviet Communist Party. The two made the trip soon after they both left UCD. Tony was very disillusioned with what he saw of the communist regime. One of the things that coloured his view was when he saw that there was one set of well-filled shops for the tourists and another set of much inferior shops for the locals. According to John, Tony was very critical of this – he thought it wrong that the regime treated its own people in this way. Part of the reason for this two-tier system, of course, was to earn precious foreign hard currency from the tourists. But the anecdote illustrates that Tony, the socialist, did not suspend his critical faculties, in contrast to the tendency of many on the Left at the time to do just that.

HARD WORK

It is one thing to have political views, it is another to be able to make them count in some way, especially for an Independent. Without the structure of a political party, Tony had to work hard to have an impact. Fortunately, he was not afraid of hard work. His family and his early political experience had taught him its value. The special insecurity of life as an Independent TD also lent an extra edge to his motivation for hard graft.

A big part of Tony's impact was down to his relentless dedication and good organisation. And he was often not best pleased if people around him did not measure up. 'He was awfully well organised and expected you to turn up,' Liz Doyle observes. Fergus McCabe describes him as:

immensely committed, never half-hearted, very professional. He was totally reliable, very competent, capable. He was very dedicated to fairness. He gave a hundred percent to fighting injustice. He was very passionate, which sometimes might spill over into moments of narkiness with his associates.

He had a strongly ingrained work ethic, undoubtedly acquired, at least in part, through the example of his mother. Seamus Martin, the former *Irish Times* journalist gave a glimpse of Tony's work ethic in his account of Irish observers in the first fully democratic post-apartheid elections in 1994 in South Africa – these were the first multi-racial elections since the establishment of the apartheid regime in 1948. Tony was one of the Irish group in the international corps of parliamentary observers who were to scrutinise the workings of the election to ensure fair play and the legitimacy of the process. Unlike one unnamed Irish senior politician who arrived with his golf clubs and expressed a wish not to serve in black areas, Tony and Nora Owen (the former Fine Gael Minister) were the two Irish politicians who impressed Seamus Martin most with their application to the task.[4]

Tony always, of course, took a very 'hands-on' approach to electoral campaigning and was not shy about shinning up and down ladders to place (often recycled) posters on lampposts. His willingness to work hard also extended to getting his hands dirty – sometimes quite literally. A city-wide campaign against bin collection charges led to a huge pile-up of rubbish outside a new apartment block close to residents in East Wall, and this was causing some aggravation for the immediate locals. Being the attentive public representative he was, Tony saw the need to make a tangible response to their concerns, thus a group of Tony's workers arrived to move the rubbish to waste ground up the road. The local people spotted Tony in the group playing his part in the removal of the offending material. Here was action speaking a thousand words. The admiring locals instantly became longterm voters for Tony and told the story to all who would listen.[5]

Tony worked hard, and he was also disciplined and well organised. As Mick Rafferty puts it, Tony had patience, the patience for the hard-grinding graft, the commitment to see an issue through, whatever it took. Council officials said to Mick, when he became a councillor in Tony's place, that Tony would 'not let things go', he would 'hound' people until he got satisfaction. He rarely trusted others in his organisation to be as attentive to detail as he was himself. In modern parlance, he could be a bit of a 'control freak' about the minutiae of electoral campaigns. He would even coach activists in how precisely to post an election leaflet through a letter box so that it landed the right way up on the doormat inside. Those who have not pushed election leaflets through countless letterboxes with their finger-hunting spring-loaded actions, or those who have not heard growling dogs jumping at the letter box from the other side, may underestimate the demands on canvassers of this commitment to these minutiae of electioneering. But it was also true that it was this attention to detail that helped Tony to withstand the power of the formidable party electoral machines that were ranged against him in each election.

Valerie Smith, his Dáil secretary in the latter years, found Tony to be extremely hard-working. He went for his lunch every day at two o'clock after Valerie came back from her lunch-break. This meant he could cover the phones while Valerie was away. At 5.00pm each day when Valerie finished work, Tony's Dáil office number would be transferred to his mobile so that calls to the office could still be picked up. These examples show how his work dominated Tony's life. This was partly his own 'addiction' to the compelling nature of the work, but it also reflected his sense of the insecurity of life as an Independent TD in a multi-seat constituency.

His desire to be elected – and his strong competitive streak – helped to drive his motivation and his work rate. But there was also a fear of failure.

Máirín de Burca, a former associate from Sinn Féin, turned journalist, wrote a broadly fair and neutral piece about Tony as councillor, four months after he was first elected:

> **There is no doubt that he is fiercely ambitious and that a seat in parliament is one of his ultimate goals, but there is equally no doubt but that he is terrified of being associated with failure. His refusal to become involved in the IRSP, even though his admiration for Costello as a political leader verged on deification, and his pussyfooting around the edges of SLP, argue a caution that could either make him or break him.[6]**

In retrospect, this is quite an astute assessment. It is likely that Tony would admit to having been fearful of electoral failure. He was driven by political conviction, but also by this fear. Two years ahead of an election, he would give an hour or more every morning to walking some part of his electoral turf, canvassing and glad-handing the voters.[7] Despite his high profile, political insecurity made him very sensitive to media coverage and to how his actions might be represented or perceived. Christy Burke recalls what Tony found as a potential nightmare experience politically: they were both part of a delegation representing Dublin City Council at an event in Japan around 1995. Tony enjoyed being part of foreign delegations, but was also acutely aware that these trips might easily be misinterpreted by his voters. Christy and Tony were joined by the then Lord Mayor of Dublin, Sean D Dublin Bay Loftus. Somehow, word from Ireland filtered back to the three of them that their trip was attracting a lot of interest from the Pat Kenny radio show. Loftus's wife rang the show to put their side of the case and argue for the importance of the delegation, which was a bit of a double-edged sword since it gave the issue a whole lot more oxygen. Tony survived the episode electorally but it made him even more sensitive about the fragility of his political reputation.

Tony was very conscious too of how precarious his status as an elected politician was – 'He never took a single vote for granted,' as Philip Boyd put it. He was critical of fellow politicians on the Left, who, he thought, dissipated their energy and political base by being too indiscriminate in their willingness to support a series of causes. He had warned Joe Higgins, the high-profile Socialist Party TD for Dublin West for 2002-07, of the importance of serving his own electorate as well as the wider causes he supported, if he wanted to retain his seat. Tony's advice proved prophetic. Joe was a willing speaker at meetings for a host of causes – but he did lose his seat in the 2007 election only to regain it in 2011.

A final example of Tony's work ethic was the fact that he actually had written questions to be answered in the Dáil on 2 December 2008, only a month before he died, when his illness was very advanced.

INNER CITY ISSUES

Tony engaged with many issues of importance to his local area over his career. In the very early days, he focused almost instinctively on issues that he had a direct feel for – housing, education and youth facilities. He felt strongly about housing from his time growing up in the inner city. He was well versed in education from his time as a teacher and from his conviction about its importance, first picked up from his mother. Linked to his interest in education was his concern to support and promote positive opportunities for local young people through sport, recreation, youth clubs and holidays in the countryside. He devoted himself to helping a range of such groups: the Adventure Sports Project, Belvedere Football Club, and local Neighbourhood Youth Projects. Many of the problems and needs he highlighted were not unique to the inner city – his case was that the scale and intensity of need were different there and required a special response. He had a strong argument. The historic neglect of the area, and its economic and social decline were best symbolised in the run-down state of the property managed by its biggest estate owner and landlord, Dublin Corporation. The housing stock and its management were a primary focus for Tony in his early political career. Housing, education, and youth facilities were issues that Tony was at home with from the outset and which he engaged with at some level throughout his time in politics. He had very visible success on the housing front with the provisions in the Gregory Deal, and while the Deal did not survive, its impact on housing development in the inner city was clear, with many spanking new houses appearing and setting a trend for much-improved Council houses throughout the area. On other fronts, he also registered successes too, but not always with such dramatic evidence. Over time, he became involved in various issues as they asserted themselves – the drugs and crime problem was the most notable. Another cause was that of the street traders in the centre city, which was a quintessential local issue. Then there were various environmental safety concerns that surfaced from time to time. The thread connecting Tony's approach to all these issues was his insistence that officialdom in its different forms addressed the special needs of the inner city.

Tony used a variety of ways to exert influence at local level and more widely. He attended endless meetings in the inner city with local residents and service providers, but there were also meetings with relevant municipal or national authorities. There were speeches in Dáil Éireann and elsewhere; there were countless media interviews. There were articles in the press – national and local – there were letters to editors sounding off on issues; there were many letters supporting grant applications or the pleas of individuals or organisations seeking to be heard by powerful decision makers. But he also devoted his time in the cause of the projects serving young people, putting in the hours driving groups to their destination in his spare time, helping renovate premises, attending planning meetings and so on.

In each issue, Tony would seek to highlight how the interests of the locals were often overlooked by the more powerful interests of others. Tony aimed to tackle inadequate responses and ingrained neglect on the part of outsiders. But he also sought to challenge low expectations on the part of local people. He often helped them remember they were entitled to better – better education, better economic opportunities, better environmental safety. Tony saw an area trapped in a vicious circle of neglect, poor standards, poor attitudes and poor expectations. He also saw how all the issues were intertwined – it was not one thing *or* the other. There had to be progress on every front. There could be no concessions in the struggle to stop the inner city being treated as a 'dump', literally and figuratively, whether in the case of defaulting tenants of the City Council, or of unregulated environmental waste. In many cases, fault lines in policies were more sharply evident in the inner city as conditions that had been allowed to accumulate there over time, and the lack of attention to the needs and concerns of the people, meant that the physically poor state of infrastructure and the environment symbolised a more general malaise than elsewhere.

Reflecting on his approach to politics a couple of years after being elected to the Dáil, Tony said:

> **I don't see myself as a political party … I see myself as a political activist, elected to the Dáil to do that on a fulltime basis.**[8]

He went on to acknowledge that his status as an elected TD was not without complexity:

> **My politics were always anti-establishment, but having been elected I'm now in the establishment. It's very confusing really. In some ways, it's impossible to reflect on what I'm doing fully. I'm just carrying activism to an extreme, twelve hours a day, five days a week.**[9]

CHAPTER 6

Tackling Drugs and Crime

The drugs problem in the north inner city – and beyond – exploded during Tony Gregory's time in politics. The former Sinn Féin activist Christy Burke, who since childhood had been a resident of the flats complex in Hardwicke Street, near Temple Street hospital, recalls the emergence of a heroin epidemic in the flats there from 1979. By then it had become, in his words, a case of 'heroin supermarkets' in the flats.[1] Things got so bad that the Jesuit priest Fr Jim Smyth, who lived in the flats, came to Christy to speak to him in his capacity as a member of Provisional Sinn Féin saying: 'I don't agree with the Provos, but we need your help. Your mother lives here, you live here.' Fr Smyth was a very humble and quiet Kerryman, with a deep and thoughtful approach to his ministry. He had worked in Hong Kong in earlier years, and on arriving back in Ireland had been assigned to teach Latin in Belvedere College; he also served as chaplain of the Belvedere Youth Club. Through this and other experiences in the inner-city community, he had become committed to a deeper engagement with the community in the flats, and decided to take up residence there. Christy Burke responded to his request by agreeing to do something, but also by saying that they should bring Tony Gregory on board. Foreshadowing the emergence later of the Concerned Parents Against Drugs (CPAD) movement in St Teresa's Gardens flats complex on Dublin's southside, and elsewhere, Fr Smyth's efforts led to the convening of two open-air meetings in the Hardwicke Street complex in 1982. Andre Lyder, who wrote a history of the anti-drug movement in Dublin working-class communities, suggested playfully that Fr Smyth 'holds the distinction of being the first "concerned parent"'.[2]

The drugs issue was to become a major part of Tony's political work for the rest of his career. While drugs began to emerge as an issue from 1979 in certain flats complexes, it was in the 1981 to 1982 period that things were really hotting up on the drugs front. It soon became clear, however, that officialdom was blissfully unaware of the situation, and not desperately anxious to become aware. But various efforts were being made to highlight the issue and the shortfall in response. One example concerns the current author, who had some years earlier held an Eastern Health Board social-work post in the north inner city, and wrote a letter to *The Irish Times,* published on 27 November 1981, which questioned claims made at a Council of Europe meeting by Donal Creed, Minister of State at the Department of Health, and Joe O'Rourke, Assistant Secretary at the Department of Health, that the heroin abuse problem in Ireland had 'stabilised'. I argued that the view that the problem had 'stabilised' was 'only understandable in terms of an ignorance, complacency or denial' about the problem and was 'seriously at odds with the experience of concerned workers close to the "street" in Dublin'.

The spread of heroin was to have a very negative impact on inner-city communities. It impacted on individuals, on families and on neighbourhoods. It is difficult for outsiders to comprehend the sheer scale of the problem and the depth of its impact in a relatively compact area. This comment by a local activist helps to bring home the point:

> At the Mass they asked people to put a candle on the altar for anyone who had a person died either from overdosing or AIDS during the year. There were 56 candles on the altar ... which is more than one every week dying of AIDs or an overdose.[3]

Right: A Socialist Labour Party poster advertising a local meeting on the housing issue, which was very close to Tony's heart all his political life.

Below: Negotiating the famous Gregory Deal in March 1982: (*left to right*) Mick Rafferty, Tony, Fergus McCabe, Charles Haughey, leader of Fianna Fáil, in the Gregory camp's temporary office at 20 Summerville Place (*Source: Alan Lund*)

Above: Tony, the Community candidate, and his team, running their campaign from the front room in Tony's home: (*left to right*) Seanie Lamb, Philip Boyd, Anne Smith, Noel Gregory, Tony. Note the constituency map. (*Source: Derek Speirs*)

Below: The negotiating team for the Gregory Deal: (*left to right*) Fergus McCabe, Tony, Noel Gregory, Mick Rafferty. (*Source: Derek Speirs*)

Right: An election leaflet for the young candidate in Dublin North Central.

Below: Near the Five Lamps, newly elected TD Tony Gregory with Charles Haughey, who served as the official starter of a sponsored cycle to Kilnacrott. Tony, in his regular gear on a regular bike, led the field home!

Independent Community Candidate
in North Central
TONY GREGORY
VOTE GREGORY [1]
The Community Candidate with the RECORD to prove it

Why vote **TONY GREGORY** for
East Wall - North Strand ?

Above: Tony Gregory TD being interviewed on his first day in the Dáil, 9 March 1982, with his brother Noel (centre) and Fergus McCabe (behind his left shoulder).
(*Source: Derek Speirs*)

Right: Tony outside the front door of the Gregory home at Sackville Gardens.

Right: A press conference highlighting the issue of the victimisation of street traders.

Below: A demonstration in support of the release of Tony from Mountjoy Jail, where he was imprisoned for his actions on behalf of street traders, passes St Stephen's Green. (*Source: Derek Speirs*)

Opposite: Tony on his release from Mountjoy Jail where he spent two weeks as a result of his actions in support of street traders. (*Source: The Irish Times*)

Above: Tony lends his support to a group of nurses in St Stephen's Green on Daffodil Day, in aid of the Irish Cancer Society.

Below: Tony in the Basin Lane Corporation Flats complex in inner-city Dublin. (*Source: Tony O'Shea*)

Two proud Dubs, both now deceased: Tony with Ronnie Drew of The Dubliners.

Often the people who became dependent were those with other difficulties already and therefore with less resources to find alternative ways of coping with life's pressures. In its cruel way, heroin appeared to make things better, but it mostly made things worse. The physical and psychological dependence made it vital for the individual to find the next 'hit', and to find the money by whatever means to buy it. This usually meant petty crime, often against those who were also poor, or at least within easy range of the daily routine of the user. Most of this petty crime was highly opportunistic – there was little high-level planning. It was more a case of: I need the money. Who can I see who has money or some goods that I can convert into money for a fix? Besides the afflicted individual there were those around them who got drawn into the web, as fellow users or as family members who were horrified by what was going on and who often found themselves in terrible dilemmas about whether or not to try to find money to pay off fines or debts that had been accumulated. They wanted to help, but quickly realised that many forms of help might only lead the person affected to stay involved with the whole scene. And they also came to appreciate how dreadfully difficult it was to break away from that scene because of the dependence not only on the substance, but also on the lifestyle.

Drugs were illegal, so the demand for them gave an opening to criminals to provide them. Drugs were highly profitable to sell, so the stakes were high. Violence quickly came into play to ensure payment of debt, to defend the territory of the supplier who wanted exclusive 'rights' in their turf, to ensure silence and compliance with the interests of the criminal in their sphere of influence, to promote an aura of invincibility, and to protect over-blown egos from perceived slights. This made the zone of operation hazardous for all involved, even for those who really were only onlookers. The threat of violence bred fear and intimidation, probably some of the worst and least recognised effects of large-scale illicit drug use. As Tony put it:

I do know that in the initial stages of the heroin thing the most prevalent reaction was one of fear. The people who were involved were known to be heavies. And people were afraid they'd be burnt out of their flats. They were afraid for their kids' sake.[4]

In such a climate, it was to take a lot of physical and moral strength over the years for Tony to speak out against serious players in the drugs trade.

In January 1982, community activists convened a meeting about the drugs issue in the North Star Hotel in Amiens Street in the north inner city. It was attended by representatives of local communities across Dublin, and by Tony (then a councillor) and by TD Michael O'Leary. It was to be the first of many gatherings in the community on the issue of drugs in the coming years.

After his election to the Dáil and the Gregory Deal in February 1982, Tony secured a meeting with Michael Woods, the new Minister for Health, in May. The meeting was attended by a number of parents and professionals from Tony's constituency who sought to impress upon the Minister the seriousness of the unfolding drug situation. There was a low-key response a few months later, when the Medico-Social Research Board were commissioned to conduct a study to attempt to measure the extent of drug use in the inner city. Tony continued to take every opportunity to make drugs a major issue. At a City Council Finance Committee meeting in October 1982, Tony reported concern at the growth of heroin in the city centre.[5] In his column in the short-lived national *Daily News* newspaper in the same month, Tony also expressed alarm at the rise of heroin use in his constituency and the apparent failure of the Gardaí to respond effectively.[6]

In April 1983 David Nowlan, the health correspondent of *The Irish Times*, leaked findings of the study commissioned by Health Minister Michael Woods the previous September.[7] Conducted by Dr John Bradshaw, from the Medico-Social Research Board, and Fr Paul Lavelle, a local curate from Lourdes Parish, Sean McDermott Street, the study findings revealed high levels of heroin use in the north inner city: in the year prior to the study, 10 percent of 15 to 24-year-olds had used heroin, 12 percent for 15 to 19-year-olds, and 13 percent of girls aged 15 to 19.[8] These were staggering percentages, far ahead of what would have been expected in this or any other community in the country.

Tony was certainly one of those ahead of the game in spotting heroin as the scourge it was to become, but he faced a very real challenge in getting the establishment to take it seriously. His long campaign on drugs issues took considerable personal courage. It entailed confronting, at different points, the threat to communities posed by self-appointed drug lords, as well as senior management in the Gardaí for what he saw, at times, as the force's inadequate response to the drugs problem in the inner city. Tony decried, for many years, the force's failure to go after the people who were pushing the drugs, especially those higher up the supply chain.

Learning from the efforts of local activists in St Teresa's Gardens flats complex in Dublin 8 in the summer of 1983, an Inner City Concerned Parents Group was formed in the north central area that October. As reported by Mick Rafferty, this initiative had an impact; it did not succeed in actually removing the heroin problem, but things had improved to a point where there was 'no pushing going on from within the community'[9] – or at least that no local residents were involved in pushing drugs in the area. Tony reviewed, with satisfaction, the growth of these community efforts during 1983 to take action against local pushers, a trend evident in a number of areas – in the Liberty House flats complex, the Hardwicke Street and Dominick Street areas, and later in St Joseph's Mansions in Killarney Street. Again, he criticised the slowness of official responses, insisting that action came only after the government had been embarrassed by media coverage of local direct action.[10] At the end of February 1984, a march led by Concerned Parents Against Drugs (CPAD) to deliver a letter of protest over government inaction to the Dáil attracted three thousand people.[11] Tony later rejected the suggestion of the Fine Gael Minister for Justice, Michael Noonan, that CPAD had paramilitary involvement.[12] Tony believed that this view of the CPAD held by some in the political establishment was distracting attention from the main issue – the destructive impact of drugs in marginalised communities.

By early 1984, Tony saw some grounds for hope and he gave an upbeat assessment in a newspaper interview in which he claimed that community pressure meant that the drugs problem was 'in decline'.[13] But this assessment was to prove short-lived and over-optimistic. The story of drugs was still unfolding. Tony made a statement in the Dáil in June 1984 in the course of a debate on the Misuse of Drugs Bill in which he claimed that five young people had died as a result of heroin abuse in the previous ten days,[14] but the Labour Party's Minister for Health, Barry Desmond, disputed the figures given by Tony:[15]

Deputy Gregory referred to five deaths over a recent weekend. He said five young people died within five days. I do not have that information. The Garda Drug Squad are aware of seven deaths in the past six months and Jervis Street Hospital say there were nine deaths. It is true that three of those deaths occurred over the weekend 8-9 June. The question of heroin abuse and deaths arising therefrom must be kept in perspective. To come into this House and try to twist the facts is not effective.

But Tony stuck to his guns, claiming supporting evidence from the Jervis Street Centre and from drug workers in the inner city.[16]

Not long after this skirmish, Tony helped to launch a book on drug abuse in Dublin, *Pure Murder*, by Sue Richardson and Noreen O'Donoghue. At this event he again criticised official inaction and highlighted the absence of any provision for addicts aged between twelve and sixteen.[17] Some time later, Davy Byrne, Assistant City and County Manager, announced that high priority was to be given to evicting drug pushers from Council tenancies, a policy in support of which Tony spoke at a meeting of the

Council's Housing Committee in September.[18]

Later that year, 1984, Tony was part of a delegation from the north inner city CPAD that met with Sinn Féin in October. The purpose of the meeting was to discuss concerns about the party's perceived dominant role in the movement, which was a major theme of media coverage of the issues. Following the meeting, it appeared that Sinn Féin had decided to adopt a lower profile in CPAD activities.[19] In November, *The Irish Times* reported that Tony was 'outraged at the leniency' of a two-year sentence imposed on Kathleen Litzouw, who, as widely reported in the media, had been convicted of possessing heroin worth £138,000. The same month, at a Dáil committee meeting on crime and related issues, Tony was critical of a reported comment by the then Deputy Garda Commissioner that drug abuse was on the decline.[20]

By March 1985, the issue of drug dealing in working-class areas was still very live. CPAD held a march through Dublin city centre and Tony was among the marchers, who came from a range of areas in the city.[21] By the summer, thirty-two groups from Tallaght and Ballybrack, as well as areas throughout the inner city and out to Ballymun, were affiliated to the central committee of CPAD.[22] Barry Desmond, as Minister for Health, still took a hard line against meeting CPAD because of his view that they had been contaminated by Sinn Féin, even where these Sinn Féin representatives had been democratically elected. Revealingly, although drugs were a major scourge during his five years as Minister for Health, and despite the fact that he steered the Misuse of Drugs Bill through the Dáil as Minister, Desmond did not give the drugs issue *any* mention in his subsequent political memoir.[23] Desmond was a very seasoned political operator and it says a great deal that such an experienced politician, and a Labour TD to boot, does not mention drugs. This is especially so given that this was such a live issue in poorer parts of his own constituency in Dún Laoghaire, as well as in poorer urban areas in many parts of the greater Dublin region and beyond.

In a way, this gives a glimpse of the gap that had opened up between mainstream politicians – even those from the broad Left family – and the experience of working-class or poor communities. This was a gap that Ruairi
Quinn acknowledged in his memoir, and a gap that Tony, among a small
number, was determined to try to fill.

In 1985, Tony joined in calls for action on racketeering and its effects on
small businesses.[24] City councillors were expressing concern at how criminal elements seemed to be seeking to fill a vacuum when insurance companies would refuse to offer cover to small businesses in areas with a high
rate of social problems. Criminals would 'offer' such businesses 'protection'
for a regular 'fee'. Those who refused might find their premises bombed or
damaged. There had been three explosions in the period prior to one of the
City Council debates on this issue. The councillors' comments suggested
this trend was relatively new, and not confined to inner city Dublin alone.

By the late 1980s, HIV/AIDS had emerged as a major health issue, and it
had a bearing on the drugs issue as the transmission of HIV/AIDS occurred,
in some cases, through the sharing of needles among intravenous drug
users.[25] This led to a subtle shift in drug policies, with more attention being
paid to harm-reduction strategies: if it proved impossible to stop individuals
using drugs, a harm-reduction approach would seek to promote awareness
and conditions conducive to less risky drug use.

On the drugs front, Tony employed a number of approaches on an ongo-
ing basis: he supported community activism against drugs; he frequently
tried to raise public awareness on the issue by writing pieces in various
newspapers with readerships as diverse as the *Sunday World* or *The Irish
Times*; he used his platform as a public representative to argue for raising
the game in terms of how the various arms of the public service responded
to the challenges. Significantly, he also wanted the assets of drug criminals
hunted down. But, overall, his analysis was disarmingly simple and clear:
'The gateway to heroin is social disadvantage. Heroin didn't emerge in any

of the affluent parts of Dublin for very obvious reasons. There's a direct link between disadvantage and hard drug abuse.'[26] Tony's choice of the word 'gateway' here is interesting, since it echoes the phrase frequently used to describe cannabis as a 'gateway drug', but this contested idea puts more emphasis on substances than on social conditions in the growth of drug use, a viewpoint that Tony challenged, certainly in relation to disadvantaged communities. Fergus McCabe argues strongly that Tony quickly reached a fuller analysis of responses needed to the drug problem that went far beyond the simple 'Pushers Out' attitude. He became deeply involved in a raft of policy level efforts across policing, service coordination and development, rehabilitation and so on.

In the Dáil debate on The Proceeds of Crime Bill 1996, Tony emphasised the multi-faceted nature of his desired approach to drug problems. In his view, responses were often too one-dimensional, relying too much on the legal system. He stressed the need to recognise the role of community groups that were fighting the drug problem alone and the need to provide treatment support facilities in areas of major heroin addiction.

> **Resources must be invested in disadvantaged areas in Dublin ... I drew the attention of the House to a disadvantaged area in the north inner city where the Department of Education under the present Minister is reducing the allocation of teachers to schools. The measures being debated in the House today will be ineffective because a reduction in the allocation of such resources fuels social disadvantage and that leads to heroin addiction.[27]**

CRIMINAL ASSETS BUREAU

During the early 1990s, Tony worked with Fergus McCabe through the Inner City Organisations Network (ICON) to set up the Inter Agency Drugs Project (IADP). The aim was to bring together representatives of the Revenue Commissioners, the Investigation Branch of the Department of

Social Welfare, the Department of Justice, the Garda Drug Unit, politicians and the community. Tony said that while the agencies eventually agreed to cooperate, they had opposed the idea of combining their efforts in a single unit. He also said it took him two years to forge the working group, using the powers already available to them, to go after the assets of the major drug dealers who had re-emerged.

In the Dáil, Tony sought to persuade Ruairi Quinn, Minister for Finance, and Nora Owen, Minister for Justice, of the merits of the concept of what was eventually to emerge as the Criminal Assets Bureau (CAB). At the Dáil Sub-Committee on Drugs (formed at Tony's proposal) Tony asked whether the Revenue Commissioners had gone after the assets of drug dealers he named and got the answer that everything possible was being done and that a new integrated agency was not required.[28] By 1995, things had deteriorated considerably. Tony grew ever more angry, frustrated at the lack of a serious, coherent, integrated response to the drug problem across government, and especially across the criminal justice system.[29]

A dramatic crime was to bring the drugs issue into very sharp political focus. On 26 June 1996, crime reporter Veronica Guerin was shot dead by a gunman on a motorbike while she was stopped at traffic lights near Dublin in her car. She had long been 'in the face' of the criminal fraternity and had been wounded in an earlier incident that had been seen as a warning to her to back off. Characteristically, she had, instead, re-doubled her efforts at exposing what was going on. Tony was very shocked by her killing.[30] Her death received huge coverage nationally and internationally. It provoked widespread shock and revulsion, both with the public and the political establishment. It finally led to the passage of legislation for the establishment of the Criminal Assets Bureau, which allowed the confiscation of unexplained assets of criminals, including major drug dealers.

Such was the impact of Guerin's killing nationally and internationally, that a film of her life, *Veronica Guerin*, directed by Joel Schumacher, appeared in 2003, with the Australian film star, Cate Blanchett, receiving very positive reviews for her portrayal of Veronica. Tony was delighted to be featured as a character in the film, and to be credited with pushing for the CAB. He was, however, mildly miffed that his character wore a tie![31]

While not receiving a lot of credit for it, Tony had the satisfaction of leading on the case for the establishment of the Criminal Assets Bureau. This issue of criminal drug-related assets had been a consistent focus of Tony's since his first days in the Dáil. He said:

> It has always struck me that when members of one criminal family who are almost synonymous with the drug problem began to buy big houses in the Dublin mountains, obviously from the proceeds of their ill-gotten gains, the Revenue Commissioners should have taken action. That would have been a way to get at them. One of the first parliamentary questions I put down on being elected was to the Minister for Finance. I named the person, who has left the country since but who still owns a house in the Dublin mountains. I asked the Minister to ensure that the Revenue Commissioners would take action against such people. The answer I got was that it was a matter for the Revenue Commissioners and that the Minister had no responsibility.
>
> I raise it again because many of the people involved in heroin pushing have been investing their gains from it in business and in property. The Revenue Commissioners have a very important role to play in dealing with this and I suggest that they should draw up some programme of action in company with the Garda. If that is not done those who gain from the drugs trade will grow more powerful and it will become increasingly difficult to deal with them.[32]

He also had called for what turned into CAB in an article he wrote in *The Irish Times* in 1995.[33] Although he had been working behind the scenes on this issue for a number of years, he never really got proper public acknowledgement for this. David Norris was one of the few who consistently sought to give him the credit for proposing the original idea for the Criminal Assets Bureau long before it was finally established in 1996.[34] At other points, Nora Owen, former Fine Gael Minister for Justice, and Dermot Ahern, Fianna Fáil Minister, also went on the record to acknowledge his key role in its establishment.

In the weeks following Veronica Guerin's murder, a public meeting was held in the parish hall in Sean McDermott Street in the north inner city on Thursday, 22 August. It had been arranged three weeks before by ICON. Newspaper reports claimed that two IRA members and some of the local drug dealers were among the five to six hundred reported to be present. The night before the planned meeting, three drug dealers were arrested outside Mountainview Court flats complex on Summerhill. The arrests took place in front of a crowd, and in the charged atmosphere that ensued, some local young people set fire to a car belonging to one of the arrested dealers. The Gardaí dispersed the people who had gathered, using a baton charge led by a group of Gardaí in riot gear. This was not a promising prelude to the meeting the next evening. In the now fraught climate, the organisers decided the meeting would be confined to residents and the media, with no Gardaí present. There was to be one exception made, however, for a Garda who still *did* command local trust and so, despite the tensions, the head of the local drug unit, Detective Sergeant John O'Driscoll, was accorded a respectful hearing at the public meeting the next evening. He expressed frustration with the courts and how they dealt with cases brought to them. Tony claimed that unless the system responded more effectively, there was a real risk of vigilantism taking hold. At this meeting, Tony famously named leading pushers, some to their faces as they sat at the meeting. This was a dramatic and courageous act. After the meeting, there was a symbolic march through the local streets to the junction of Buckingham Street and Sean McDermott Street, then a hot spot for public drug dealing. The crowd saw themselves 'reclaiming the land' there that night as Christy Burke put it (the junction is now the site of a moving local memorial to the all too many young people who died from drugs – see below).

Four weeks later, in a city-wide culmination of local protests, there was an anti-drugs march through the city centre expressing the anger and frustration of inner-city communities in the face of the drug problem blighting their areas and the feeble official response. The march earned a thoughtful, approving and lengthy editorial the next day in *The Irish Times*. The paper's editor at the time was Conor Brady, who had written pieces on inner-city issues in the past. The editorial acknowledged as 'serious and well-grounded' the concerns that these protests might open the way to vigilantism or to Sinn Féin infiltration. However, the piece also insisted that such concerns

> **must not be allowed to obscure the real importance of what is taking place on the streets of our capital city; tens of thousands of people are angry and exasperated. Many have lost family, friends, and relatives to the drug dealers. Many watch in dismay as the dealers ply their trade on the balconies and on the streets around them. All share a belief they have been left to their own devices. They have no faith in the ability and commitment of the Garda to combat the problem, still less in the government and main political parties.[35]**

By December, *The Star*, an avowedly tabloid newspaper in the British tradition of red tops and modelled on its British parent, published an extensive feature based, it claimed, on a Garda intelligence report that it had obtained. The gist of the piece was that up to thirty-five IRA men were active in inner-city communities in their version of the fight against drugs.[36] While it is impossible to verify such assertions, given their nature and provenance, the relevance is that, as fact or propaganda, the piece reflected a popular perception at the time.

Despite the efforts to combat and prevent drug use, the facts remained daunting as to the extent of the problem. Research by Catherine Comiskey estimated that there were over 13,600 opiate users aged 15 to 54 in Dublin in 1996[37], a population similar to that of a medium-sized Irish town such as Athlone.

Christmas 1996 was to see the first of an annual series of powerfully symbolic Christmas trees erected on the junction of Buckingham Street and Sean McDermott Street. These trees were to represent those local young people whose lives had been lost to drug addiction. The tree was to be a collective source of light and comfort for family members who survived and endured. Later this site was turned into a permanent memorial: in the year 2000, a locally commissioned sculpture, 'Home', by Leo Higgins, was erected there. The sculpture was to be a symbol of hope in the face of the misery wreaked locally by drugs. Among the relatives bereaved by drug use was Bernie Howard, who recalls her part in the preparation for the sculpture:

> It was very hard for me that day, when I went over to Leo's foundry where the memorial was being put together. We were told to bring something personal belonging to our lost children. I brought a miraculous medal that my Stephen wore around his neck and a small pillbox with other holy medals. It was a very, very sad occasion. I just placed his belongings in a bag, along with the personal effects of the other children being remembered. It all went into the melt; there wasn't a dry eye in the foundry that day. When I pass by the memorial now, I look at the flame and I know a part of my son is in it.[38]

By the following August, there was a somewhat more encouraging picture. Tony was being quoted as saying that the dealers 'have not been completely driven out, but it is a total transformation from a year ago when there was open dealing of anything you wanted on the footpaths and traffic islands.'[39] Another editorial in *The Irish Times* cheered on the progress, noting that a combination of local activism and the establishment of the Criminal Assets Bureau had produced, at the very least, 'grounds for optimism'.[40]

Tony did not rest on his laurels. He was still plugging away on the issue long after the CAB's establishment, attempting to get more effective implementation. In 2007, he spoke in the Dáil against the failure to move effectively against the middle-ranking distributors of drugs, whose extravagant lifestyle without sanction was drawing more young people into this type of crime.

For some years, I have been seeking a review or redeployment of the Criminal Assets Bureau so that it would have units operating in the communities worst affected by drug crime. I am calling for this because I see little evidence that drug dealers at local level – the middle range that organises distribution – are in any significant way directly affected by the Criminal Assets Bureau's work. In my experience, they are not cut off social welfare and do not have their assets, such as cars and jeeps, confiscated. The fact that this does not happen attracts other young people into drug crime, which is why it is spiralling. We need to know why this is not happening. We need to provide the Criminal Assets Bureau with the legal backing and resources to make it happen. That is what the Criminal Assets Bureau was set up to do. It is timely to have an in-depth review ... we must remember that since the bureau was established, drug crime has spiralled out of control, not just in Dublin but throughout the country. There is a message in that development.[41]

The Minister for Justice at the time was the Progressive Democrat leading light and formidable barrister, Michael McDowell – the PDs were the proudly ideological storm-troopers for free-market economics and politics on the Irish political landscape; with an almost eerie symmetry, the rise and fall of the PDs coincided with the rise and fall of the Celtic Tiger. So McDowell was certainly not hard-wired to have a natural sympathy for Tony's take on policy issues. In answer to Tony's question on the issue in an earlier debate, the Minister said:

In recent days I took the occasion to discuss the Deputy's proposal with the Garda Commissioner at some length. He strongly advised me that there would not be an advantage to a structural re-organisation of the work of the Criminal Assets Bureau along a regional model, and he set out his reasons to me at some length ...[42]

Tony tried again:

I again ask the Minister, if targeting the assets of drug crime is the way forward, does he agree it would be a good idea to target those assets at local level. With the Leas Ceann Comhairle's permission, I will give a brief example of what I mean. This is one of many. A young couple was raided in a private apartment where drugs were found and they were charged. One of them will take the rap. Currently, the partner, who is on social welfare, who has a rent allowance and who drives a blacked-out jeep, has just returned from a skiing holiday, and has had expensive cosmetic surgery – there are a range of other matters I do not have time to mention here. At the lower to middle level in the drugs trade nothing is being done about any of those matters, for instance, claiming social welfare while being clearly caught in possession of a large amount of drugs and having assets available to them which they clearly could not have on a social welfare income. That is the scenario that fuels the drug crime gangs whose members are killing one another every couple of weeks in this city. That is the way the gangs build up.

The Criminal Assets Bureau, according to the debates in this House and elsewhere, was set up to target people like that, whether through their social welfare payments, their jeeps, their expensive holidays, etc. The bureau is not doing that at local level. I am not interested in whether the bureau is centralised or localised. I am interested in operatives targeting assets of people involved in drugs at local level. It is not happening.

Having listened to Tony's argument, McDowell responded much more favourably. He commented:

I have a good deal of sympathy with the point Deputy Gregory made. From recent accounts given to me of places to which the Garda has gone where crime has been committed or where people have fled following crimes, I have been surprised by the accumulation of physical possessions such as flat-screen televisions in various bedrooms where there does not seem to be a support base for it. I take Deputy Gregory's point that in such cases there should be a follow-up. Those involved should not simply note these matters and leave the house. Somebody should return to take what appear to be proceeds of crime, directly or indirectly, into possession. That is a matter which I will raise with the Commissioner.

I am not suggesting to the Deputy that all is perfect, nor am I stating that the CAB is perfect. Perhaps I did not fully understand the Deputy's point. I believed he was suggesting the CAB be regionalised but he is proposing to have on-the-ground asset hounds whose job it would be to sweep up assets. That is a useful suggestion. In each Garda division there is now a criminal assets profiler whose job it is to examine assets in his or her division and bring information thereon to the attention of the CAB generally. The CAB has local eyes and ears on the ground and is not working entirely within a bubble in Dublin. I would like that to be understood.

The Deputy is making a different point which I understand; it concerns the prioritisation of criminals with the jeeps, holidays and plasma televisions. Just because criminals are operating below a certain threshold does not mean action should not be taken against them. Depriving people of their assets will actually turn the tide in the war against drugs. I take the Deputy's point in this regard.

In response, Tony summarised his demand: he was calling for a 'mini-CAB'.

The simple way to achieve that is to localise or regionalise the CAB. A centralised bureaucracy inevitably deals with high profile cases and tackles the criminal with the ten big houses. It never comes to grips with those at the middle level. I do not mind what approach is taken once the job is done but the most practical approach is to localise and regionalise the centralised bureaucracy that the bureau has become.

COMMUNITY POLICING FORUM

One of the classic dilemmas for left-wing politics is how to respond to crime, or, to be more precise, the criminal. The Left has tended to be more preoccupied with the causes of crime, the Right more with the culprits who commit the crime. Tony was very clear that the underlying causes of crime had to be addressed, but he also saw the importance of recognising the victim, who in the inner city was often a fellow resident of the same area. Earlier than many on the Left, Tony was ready to call for clear measures to tackle serious persistent offenders, such as big-time drug pushers. Tony was certainly not shy about tackling crime as an issue and brought many fresh ideas to local and wider policy debates on how to deal more effectively with issues of crime. One of the recurring themes of his political effort was to highlight the impact of crime on inner-city residents and, in particular, to highlight shortcomings in the response by the Gardaí as an organisation. Over the years, his message was part of the mix that led to some reorientation by the Guards themselves. The cooperation of the public generally, and the legitimacy of the Gardaí in harder-to-police areas specifically, could no longer be taken for granted. The Gardaí had to demonstrate a responsiveness to concerns that earned this cooperation and legitimacy. For his part, also, Tony recognised increasingly the importance of a police force that commanded the trust of the community it served. He invested a lot of energy in helping to foster better relations between the Gardaí and the local communities in the inner city:

> Last night I attended a meeting in Store Street Garda station of the community policing forum in the north inner city. This is an initiative which I was involved in setting up where the local authority, the Garda drug unit and the community come together in their efforts to counter the drugs problem in the north inner city. After at least twenty-five years of a drugs plague and scourge in Dublin's north inner city, last night when the Garda drugs officer made his report of drug seizures over the past couple of

months throughout the north city area, despite all the hype we hear about cocaine being the new drug, seizures of heroin were reported everywhere, right throughout the north city ...

The national strategy includes the idea of community policing fora in every drugs task force area. Having one in the north inner city is a great help according to the local authority, Garda and community, which must be brought together if there is to be an effective approach to countering the drugs problem. I hope similar fora will be set up throughout task force areas.

Not far from Leinster House this morning, I attended a joint policing committee review, which is another strand of the strategy. I hope initiatives such as community policing fora and local authorities' joint policing committees are a step towards the democratisation of the Garda. I would like to believe that when there are directly elected mayors in some areas such as Dublin city in a few years' time, the Garda will fall under the local authorities' and mayors' remits. This may be a long way off, but it is necessary.[43]

It is worth noting that what Tony proposes is not outlandish when seen in the international context. While it is crucial to avoid policing becoming over-politicised or too identified with one set of interests, as the Northern Ireland experience has taught us, it is also clear that policing requires legitimacy which is derived in part from close engagement with the communities being policed.

The Community Policing Forum was very typical of Tony's hands-on, pragmatic, and, in the Irish context, quite innovative approach to political challenges. He recognised that crime and drugs brought major problems to local residents and had to be addressed in a number of ways. Matters would not be helped by alienation or conflict between residents and the Gardaí. As in much of his work, Tony sought to find a way to open up a space where community residents and the state services could interact constructively with each other. Tackling drugs and crime required cooperation between

the Guards and the community. Tony grasped that point early and had ideas
about how it could happen. With others from the north inner city – the
Inter-Agency Drug Project and the Inner City Organisations Network –
he generated proposals and then coaxed the various players (the Guards, the
community representatives and the City Council) into a pilot project that
very gradually moved to a point of formal establishment some three years
later. Patience was a necessary quality for Tony in his work!

When the Community Policing Forum was finally put on a formal foot-
ing, a reception was to be organised for the various VIPs to give it their
blessing. Marie Metcalfe, a newly appointed fulltime worker for the Forum,
tells an amusing story about the choice of venue for this formal launch in
October 2002. It illustrates well some of the *realpolitik* of improving com-
munity-police relations. The launch was to be attended by all kinds of local
worthies and by the Garda Commissioner Pat Byrne, the City Manager
John Fitzgerald and the ubiquitous Bertie Ahern, as Taoiseach and local
TD. A very early task for Marie was to organise the event and the first issue
was to choose a suitable venue. Many assumed that it would end up being
in a local hotel, but Marie had other ideas. Store Street Garda Station, in
the heart of the area, had just undergone a major extension and refurbish-
ment and Marie decided that this should be the venue – where else but the
local Garda Headquarters for the launch of the new Community Policing
Forum? The response was consternation among some of the locals who
were not used to socialising with Gardaí in Garda stations. Marie reckoned,
however, that curiosity would kill the cat: the idea of getting in to have a
'nosey' around the new station would prove too great to resist.

But there was one remaining difficulty before the event could go swim-
mingly. A number of the street traders confided in Marie that they would
regretfully have to send their apologies – they had arrest warrants outstanding on them in relation to earlier skirmishes with the Guards in their
campaign for their cause. In the light of this, they thought that it would be

pushing their luck to turn up to the bun-fight with the local big-wigs in the local Garda headquarters! Marie was undeterred. 'Leave it with me,' she declared, and she arranged a meeting with the local Chief Superintendent at which she extracted a discreet guarantee that the event would not be marred by any insensitive or impolitic timing in the serving of outstanding arrest warrants. Marie then managed to convince a still sceptical set of street traders that she had struck a deal for their continuing liberty and that this would hold at least until after the 'do'. The women could risk enjoying the Guards' free wine! Their presence would be yet another sign of how Tony's influence helped foster good working (and social) relations between local people and representatives of the state systems.

The Community Policing Forum launched that day was to become a template for similar developments in many communities across the country, another example of Tony's wider influence.

CHAPTER 7

• • • • • •

Other Issues

EDUCATION

Tony's first political speech in community politics was at a meeting on educational disadvantage in 1978 at Liberty Hall. By day he was teaching middle-class young people in south Dublin. By night – or in his spare time – he was fighting the cause of young people who did not have the same opportunities as the young people he taught. The venue for the meeting where Tony made his debut was highly appropriate: Liberty Hall represented an iconic site and title in the history of the Irish Left. A previous Liberty Hall on the same site had been the headquarters of the Irish Transport and General Workers' Union founded by James Larkin in 1908; it had also been the base of the Irish Citizens' Army which joined the 1916 Rebellion. Maureen O'Sullivan recalls Tony being nervous in advance of this first outing as a speechmaker in his own right. It soon became clear, however, that nerves did not dilute his conviction or clarity in public speaking.

He was to use many different platforms over the years to advance his views on reforming educational provision. Soon after that meeting, he wrote a long letter to *The Irish Times* on the theme of educational disadvantage in March 1978.[1] The letter was remarkably detailed and well informed as to the nature of the issues at stake. It was a hint of the talent that lay waiting to be tapped. The letter was responding to the outcry about the impending closure of the secondary school for middle-class girls run by the Dominican nuns and then located in Eccles Street beside the Mater Hospital. Among the arguments marshalled by opponents of the closure was the claimed impact on inner-city children. Tony pointed out, acidly, that there would be virtually no impact, since the school's seven hundred children came from fifty-four parishes around the city, but almost none of the students were from the inner city. In the very full letter, he claimed that the religious, as the overall providers of education in the area, had 'failed in their responsibility'. He argued that what was needed immediately was 'a comprehensive-type community school specifically for the north inner city along with state financed pre-schools and the re-development of local primary schools'.

This focus on education was to be a strong feature in Tony's political effort throughout his career. The importance of education was a recurring theme in interviews he did on his political priorities or concerns. It was also a constant thread in his contributions in Dáil debates. He saw failure to address the educational disadvantage in his constituency – and more widely – as being inextricably bound up with social problems such as illicit drug use. Tony's commitment to education had come from many sources – the objective needs and problems in his political heartland, his own upbringing where education was so valued, his training and experience as a teacher, as well as his socialist analysis which would place great value on public investment in educational opportunity for all.

In addition to different forms of public campaigning on educational issues, Tony also took advantage of speaking time in the Dáil to register his concerns and priorities. He saw education as the most powerful form of prevention against drugs and crime problems in the inner city and elsewhere and he took every opportunity to make his point. The following two examples of his input to the Dáil on education give a good flavour of his overall emphasis. In the Dáil on 18 November, 1998, he said:

In the two minutes Deputy Bruton agreed to share with me, I wish to make

a special case for national schools in the drugs task force areas. Those areas of extreme social disadvantage should not be assessed under national criteria on disadvantage in respect of the pupil–teacher ratio. They should be assessed as having an exceptional need and the Breaking the Cycle scheme should be expanded in national schools in those areas. Heroin is unique to those areas. The only way children who attend those schools will have any real chance of overcoming the temptation of drugs, completing second level and going on to third level is to give them an opportunity in school.

It is not a coincidence that those areas have the lowest level of access to third level education in the State. It is incredible that a Cabinet subcommittee deals with social exclusion and drugs, but an initiative has not been taken to address the problem in primary schools in those areas. The chairman of the Government's National Strategy Committee on Drugs told a Dáil committee today that education must be the first line of defence in the war against drugs. The previous Government's ministerial task force designated 12 areas in Dublin and one in Cork as drugs task force areas. The 12 areas in Dublin were heroin blackspots and required urgent attention to address social disadvantage if progress was to be made against a heroin crisis. The previous Government introduced the Breaking the Cycle scheme, which is the single most effective measure to combat social exclusion and the drugs problem. Many of the national schools in the north inner city and in the other drugs task force areas benefit greatly from that scheme and progress is being made. However, the Minister's record to date has been disastrous in this regard.

In the Dublin 1 and Dublin 7 areas, which span two heroin task force areas, no fewer than nine national schools lost teachers at the start of this school year. As a result, junior classes were maintained at Breaking the Cycle level, but senior classes had to double up. The progress that was made is now being wasted. Schools which lost teachers include those in Sheriff Street, Seán Mac Dermott Street, Hardwicke Street and O'Devaney Gardens, areas of multiple deprivation. I appeal to the Minister to reverse these losses for the reasons I outlined.

The next extract, also from a Dáil speech (1 December 2005) on the issue of a threat to educational support provision in inner city schools gives a further flavour of Tony's commitment and characteristically direct and clear argument – not to mention his swipe at the then Minister for Education, Mary Hanafin. Bear in mind that he was speaking at the height of the Celtic Tiger era, when, it seemed, the government had access to more money than it knew how to spend. Bear in mind, also, that Tony actually got on quite well with Mary Hanafin. They had served together on Dublin City Council at one point. Also, as Chief Whip of the Technical Group (2002-07) in the Dáil, Tony had reason to have a lot of dealings with the government Chief Whip who for part of that period had been Mary Hanafin. Imagine the lash of his tongue that those whom he disliked might earn!

> Last night I attended a meeting of parents and teachers in the INTO headquarters in Parnell Square. The main hall and surrounding hallways were packed with nearly 400 parents, teachers, principals, child psychologists and so on. Those attending were understandably angry at the inept approach to learning support allocation in so far as it affects small disadvantaged schools with a high level of need. Teachers and parents expressed outrage that at a time of considerable affluence critical resources are being withdrawn from these schools. These resources had begun to make a significant difference to the degree to which the schools in question could help deprived children.

> I call on the Minister to address this issue now. The level of need in each of the 14 schools must be known to her Department. If that is not the case, it is time she ensured the relevant information was made available to her. She must also defer any threat to remove resource teachers or reduce resource hours in any small disadvantaged school. Investment in alleviating educational disadvantage must involve increasing resources in inner city disadvantaged schools or it becomes meaningless. How can the Minister even countenance reducing resources in schools serving Sheriff Street,

O'Devaney Gardens, Summerhill, Ballybough and Greek Street, to mention just a few areas? Investment in schools in these areas will pay dividends in future.

If the Minister is serious about addressing disadvantage, she will meet the people on the front line of disadvantage, the principals of the inner city schools, and listen to what they have to say. Not only will she not meet them, she will not come into the House to respond to the matter I raise. She is running away from her responsibilities on this issue. She was in the coffee dock 20 minutes ago in full knowledge that I intended to raise this matter on the Adjournment, yet decided to allow another Minister to answer on her behalf. That is a disgrace and shows disrespect to the parliamentary procedures of the House.

Tony's commitment to education brought him some highs and lows. One of his proudest achievements was the eventual opening, many years after it was first mooted, of Larkin Community College in 1999 in a fine new premises on Sean McDermott Street. This was a development first agreed in the original Gregory Deal. The school materialised twenty-one years after he had first called for its development in that letter to *The Irish Times*, and seventeen years after the Gregory Deal. At the official opening Tony sat modestly in the body of the hall, no doubt enjoying the quiet satisfaction that his long-cherished dream had at last been realised.

One of his bitterest political experiences was being refused speaking time, while at an advanced stage in his terminal illness, on the educational cuts in a Dáil debate. Very controversially, in emergency budgets following the financial crash in late 2008, the government had singled out education as one of the areas in which to achieve savings. Many of the measures targeted related to educational provision in the areas of disadvantage and disability. The exclusion of Tony from an opportunity to speak on these cuts was alluded to by Maureen O'Sullivan in her tribute in the church at his funeral mass and she spoke with some bitterness on the point.

Tony's efforts in the field of education did not go unappreciated or unrecognised. In a tribute on Tony's death, John Carr, General Secretary of the Irish National Teacher's Organisation – the powerful trade union for primary teachers – credited the Gregory Deal with being the first step towards specific public measures to combat educational disadvantage. Carr said that:

> Aspects of that deal subsequently became the cornerstone of national programmes to tackle poverty and educational disadvantage ... Tony Gregory's insistence that educational investment was central to that deal had benefits not only for children in his constituency but for children nationwide.[2]

Tony would have valued such comment from an experienced and high-profile leader of the largest teacher union in the country. John Carr's comments served to underline that the Gregory Deal was not parochial but had wider national impact.

STREET TRADERS

In July 1983 six women street traders were fined for selling fruit in Henry Street, one of the great shopping streets off O'Connell Street. Their offence was not to have a license, or to be selling in an area in which street trading was illegal. The pram was crucial to the street traders' system of operating. Many of them sold their stock from bread boards laid on top of prams. The prams assisted mobility when trying to escape the attentions of any Gardaí who might appear. A quick getaway was important to avoid the risk of having valuable stock confiscated, or having valuable selling time eroded by tiresome periods trapped in Garda stations, or worse. The anthem of their cause became 'Stand by Your Pram' with apologies, of course, to Dolly Parton.

Tony responded to the fines by calling for an extension of the areas in the centre city that were licensed for street trading.[3] The Guards were acting at the behest of local business owners who did not like the presence of the street traders. Tony was not slow to highlight this point. He was critical about the difference in the way the Guards responded to street traders and drug pushers – he saw less of a clampdown on the drug pushers. He saw the issues affecting the legitimacy of the Guards in the eyes of the local community in a piece he wrote in a local magazine:

> **I want to mention something that makes me see red. It's when I hear the Gardaí whinging that they don't have community support in the Inner City. I'll just take two examples to make my point … when business firms demand Gardaí action against unfortunate street traders, the Gardaí arrive in force and bundle women and prams into paddy wagons and off to the cells in Store Street. But when tenants or priests or community workers look for help against heroin pushers, the Gardaí all but ignore them. The moral seems to be the Gardaí are a tool of the rich to be used against the community. If the Gardaí want community support in the city centre then they should act in the community interest. They could and should make heroin too hot to handle.[4]**

Later that year, Tony was reported as saying he was not 'going to be dictated to by Roches Stores (then a department store on Henry Street) or anyone else' when council officials said that business interests were objecting to the granting of more licenses to street traders.[5] Further controversy erupted that Christmas when it emerged that trading for the three Christmas weeks would now require a full annual licence costing £120 as compared with a 25p permit previously. Tony complained too that the Corporation planners were being obstructive in efforts to find suitable space for licensed trading. They had said that trading would be a traffic hazard in Cole's Lane, yet, as Tony pointed out, Cole's Lane was a pedestrian area![6] The issue was to rumble on for many years.

In January 1985, Tony and the local Garda Superintendent in the inner city attended a mass meeting on street trading. It was an issue that the Superintendent claimed was 'the bane' of his life. He said he would like to see an amicable solution as an alternative to the six hundred prosecutions he estimated were brought against street traders in 1984.[7] In July, street traders organised a protest to mark the imprisonment of three of their colleagues. Fr Michael Casey, parish priest for Lourdes parish was quoted as saying:

The Gardaí have a lot more important things to do in my estimation than pursuing a group of women who want to make a living for their families. They are being abused at present as tools of an inefficient bureaucracy and avaricious business people.[8]

Later in the month, Tony was reported as saying that while the Gardaí were 'running women traders off the streets they are not dealing with heroin pushers who are operating within a stone's throw of Store Street Station'.[9] Christy Burke recalls Tony and himself regularly being called out to represent women who had been arrested and were having their goods confiscated – no small matter for women with large families who were often merely eking out an existence. The stock for sale would vary with the seasons, with every possible commercial opportunity grasped: 'They took all the Valentine cards' would be a typical opening line in a phone call pleading for support in the face of Garda pressure.[10] By late July, Fr Michael Casey had enlisted Dublin Auxiliary Bishop, James Kavanagh, to play a mediating role between all the parties involved.[11]

Tony appeared in court on remand with five others on 30 July linked to charges of assaulting Gardaí, obstruction and threatening behaviour. The incident arose in connection with street trader protests. Tony had joined with Christy Burke, Joe Costello and others in a sit-down protest blocking the traffic in O'Connell Street. As Tony ruefully admitted to Christy later, a sit-down protest was a tactical error as it made the job of the arresting Gardaí a whole lot easier. In any case, they were all bundled into a Bedford van that then served as a Black Maria for the Guards. Tony found himself lying flat on his back with feet against the back door. As any self-respecting captive would do in such circumstances, his first instinct was to kick against the doors, only to find that they flew open! Quick as a flash, Tony was away, but was soon re-arrested.

He was subsequently sent to prison because he refused to sign a bond to keep the peace – he refused on the grounds that to do so would prevent him highlighting the rights and needs of his constituents.[12] Tony started his two-week sentence on 28 January 1986, but was sent, by Ministerial Order, directly to the more modern conditions of the Training Unit in Mountjoy Prison complex, thus avoiding an experience of the grim conditions in the main prison.[13] Christy Burke was arrested a few days later and joined Tony in the same unit. Mountjoy was familiar territory to Christy. He had served time there for membership of the IRA and was there the day in October 1973 when the IRA pulled off a famous stunt, a helicopter escape by three men from the main courtyard. (It is alleged on very good authority that one of the prison officers could be heard shouting 'shut the gates' as the helicopter with the escaped prisoners on board rose back into the sky.)

John Lonergan, the Governor of Mountjoy Prison, recognised their status as public representatives, accepted their claim to be 'political prisoners', and facilitated them in representing their constituents. However, he gave what Christy Burke describes as a 'friendly dismissal' to their bid to be released to attend a critical vote on the City Development Plan in the City Council. Meanwhile, nightly protests outside the prison Training Unit underlined the support for the cause – though local activist Seanie Lambe recalls, ruefully, that the impact of the pickets was slightly impaired given that no one could see or hear them since the unit entrance was very much hidden away down back lanes far from public view! A number of the street traders also announced that they too wanted to be imprisoned as an act of solidarity with Tony.[14]

Tony served his two weeks and after his release continued his faithful commitment to the street traders' cause. The saga dragged on for a long time but eventually he began to see results for his efforts with significant gestures made to the traders. On 2 November 1993 there was a brief ceremony out-side the ILAC Centre to mark the opening of twelve new stalls presented to the street traders by the ILAC, Roches Stores and Dunnes Stores!

The street trader cause remained a favourite issue for Tony right to the end of his career. One of his last political appearances was to record an input to the documentary by Joe Lee, 'Bananas and Breadboards', about inner-city street traders.

ENVIRONMENTAL SAFETY AND PLANNING

Tony regularly acted as an environmental watchdog at the political level in voicing the concerns of local groups on a range of issues where institu-tional powers sought to steamroll local interests. He revelled in taking on large institutional interests where he saw them imposing on local residents. One example deals with the transport of toxic chemicals by rail though his constituency to Dublin port. Another concerns the GAA and their actions in the context of the Croke Park stadium re-development. Christy Burke recalls Tony berating them at a local public meeting at which Danny Lynch, the GAA Public Relations Officer, was present. Criticising their lack of consideration for and communication with local residents, Tony accused the GAA of acting like 'urban terrorists'. Lynch took it on the chin, not that he had much choice! On match days, Tony was generally not to be found cheering Dublin from the terraces on Hill 16 – he was more likely to be outside the ground spending his time checking that everything pos-sible was being done to protect local residents from unnecessary hassle or disruption.

Josephine Henry was an urban planner working with Community Tech-nical Aid on a project advising the local community on their submission to a planning hearing in relation to the development of the Smithfield area in North West inner Dublin. She recalls Tony's contribution and approach:

The day of the hearing came and Tony showed his true political mettle; when questioned about the need 'for an economic quantum development' by the hearing inspector, he replied that he was there to show development affected people and their neighbourhoods, not making an argument for developers.[15]

One of the more incredible proposed developments he resolutely opposed was the attempt to build underground gas storage caverns in Dublin Bay. Philip Boyd recounts a tale on this front that caused Tony much mirth. When he was a councillor, Tony got a call one day from Tom Roche Senior, promoter of the controversial gas storage scheme. He asked to meet Tony for lunch to discuss the project, and Tony agreed. The venue turned out to be the St Stephen's Green Club. Roche made clear he was looking for support for his project. At the end of the lunch he handed Tony a cheque and told him that he could make it out to whomever he wanted. Tony took the cheque, donated it to the Cavan Centre (Kilnacrott), and then voted against the project when it was presented to the City Council.

In 1986, Tony highlighted the lackadaisical approach taken by Dublin Corporation to the storage of asbestos waste in Mayor Street, a stone's throw from the Sheriff Street flats complex. He reported that there were 'now more than twenty tons of the asbestos packed in double plastic bags and stored in two closed transport containers'. Raising this with the City Manager, he was told:

Asbestos has not been declared by the Minister for Labour to be a dangerous substance under the Dangerous Substances Act 1972 ... From a planning viewpoint there is no breach of the Planning Acts as this site has a long history of storage and warehousing.

The issue had arisen because Britain no longer accepted asbestos waste. As Tony observed:

The City Manager's reply seems to be completely out of touch with the growing public concern about asbestos waste. Britain bans it and our Corporation ignores it.'[18]

The episode highlights how badly in need of a wake-up call was senior management in the Corporation, and how detached they were from the basic interests of the ordinary citizens of the city.

REPUBLICAN ISSUES

While he was careful not to inflict his republican sympathies on an electorate that generally had other priorities, Tony remained true to his beliefs and often took the opportunity to lend support to people in the broader republican family or to republican causes. He did some work in support of the H Block cause in 1980-81. He played a significant part in trying to mediate a resolution to a hunger strike by republican prisoners of different hues in Limerick prison in September 1982.[17] David Andrews, former Fianna Fáil Minister, notes that Tony was one of the small number of politicians acknowledged by Birmingham Six member Paddy Hill, as having kept up an interest in their cause.[18] He supported Christy Burke in his early years as a local politician. He helped to promote the campaign for the release of Nicky Kelly.[19] Kelly had been sentenced in 1978 to twelve years for his alleged part in the Sallins Train Robbery. Protesting his innocence, a national campaign eventually bore fruit with Kelly's release in 1984; he later received a presidential pardon and a compensation payment of over £1 million.

Questioned on his stance on republicanism in 1985, Tony was quite forthright:

I believe that Britain is to blame for most of the violence in the North ... and I have never hesitated from using my position as a TD to spell that out ... But I am not going to stand on a platform and call on young people

to take up arms and fight against the British in the North. I will not ask people to do what I am not prepared to do myself.[20]

While he retained a quiet loyalty to republican causes, Tony also retained his critical faculties not just in relation to the exponents of socialism, but also toward the actions of those in the republican family. According to Liz Doyle, he was bitterly dismissive of the atrocities perpetrated by the Provisionals against civilians, Disparagingly dubbing those responsible for the bombing of shopping centres and such like as 'shopper bombers'.

Tony was proud of his republicanism. He often took up issues with republican links. But the pragmatist in him meant that he found a fine balance between hiding and flaunting his republican beliefs. He certainly didn't hide them, but neither did he trail them before an electorate that often had other preoccupations. If his electorate did not express republican priorities, then he felt that it was not his place as their public representative to impose these on them. He understood the basic premise of democracy. Geraldine Kennedy, later editor of *The Irish Times*, interviewed him during the Deal negotiations, and asked him how strong his republican views were at that point:

In the context of our negotiations and what is going on at the moment, they don't play a part at all. They have not arisen in any of the discussions with anybody: they didn't arise in my election literature or in the course of the campaign. I reflect the viewpoint of a large number of people who organised my campaign.[21]

But at times his republican instincts won through, as when, with Christy Burke, he abstained in the vote to elect Tomás Mac Giolla of The Workers Party as Lord Mayor of Dublin.[22] In an interview in *In Dublin* magazine, Tony revealed something of the lingering bitterness between old comrades: 'If Mac Giolla walked into me in a confined space, he'd find some way of not looking at me.'[23] The Workers Party's abandonment of its republican roots had clearly left a sour taste for Tony. He, of course, also held them responsible for collapsing the Haughey-led government whose fall meant the end of the Gregory Deal.

DUBLIN AND MONAGHAN BOMBINGS

In 1974, a loyalist bomb squad from Northern Ireland, allegedly with British security forces collusion, detonated three bombs in central Dublin. Two of the bombs exploded in the north inner city, one each in Talbot Street and Parnell Street. The third blew up just south of the river Liffey in Lincoln Place, along by the railings of Trinity College and within virtual shouting distance of the Dáil around the corner in Kildare Street. In all, thirty-three people were killed that day, the highest death toll of any day in the Troubles. Previous bombings in Dublin had caused deaths, two in December 1972 in what almost certainly was an attempt to influence voting on security legislation under debate in the Dáil on the very day; there was also one further death in a bombing in January 1973. These are episodes that remain unresolved, officially, to this day. In his speech of tribute in the Dáil marking Tony's passing, Bertie Ahern recalled how, when he was Taoiseach, Tony used to question him regularly on the issue, and how this helped to drive attention to it:

> In all the years I held that position, he came in here to question me about the ongoing work on the issue of the Dublin and Monaghan bombings. He never let an opportunity go – the questions were normally in his name or the names of other Deputies – to raise that issue. Much of the work that took place, and the motivation to continue that work and the efforts I put into continue it, were because he had raised the issue time and again, both privately and publicly, and in this House.[24]

TONY GREGORY

FOREIGN AFFAIRS

Tony took many opportunities to promote his left-wing analysis on foreign affairs. He was one of three TDs who walked out of the Dáil chamber in advance of the address to the Houses of the Oireachtas by United States President Ronald Reagan in 1984. The Workers Party TDs, Tomás Mac Giolla and Proinsias de Rossa, joined him as the three of them protested at American foreign policy.[25]

In 2005 he was part of a parliamentary delegation to Palestine that included Aengus Ó Snodaigh (Sinn Féin), John Gormley (The Green Party) and Terry Leyden (Fianna Fáil). They were shot at, causing at least one of the distinguished members to find a new facility for leaping in the air, possibly not the best form of cover under fire! On his return, Tony issued a statement that strongly reflected his unequivocal support for the Palestinian cause:

This was my second visit to the occupied territories in Palestine. My earlier visit was at the beginning of the first Intifada – in the late 1980s. Things have not improved since then; if anything, they are worse. It's only when you go there and see at first hand the deliberate policy of suppression and impoverishment of the Palestinian people that you fully appreciate the enormity of this crime against humanity. We now see the creation of apartheid regions and structures by the Israelis where settlers move in, occupy the most dominant part of an area, and build their fortified settlements, often cutting off the most arable land from the Palestinian villages and homes. Road access is blocked off in an attempt to make continued existence for the Palestinians unsustainable. A further ingredient is the construction of motorways and tunnels linking the settlements – motorways which are exclusive to the Israeli settlers with the Palestinians excluded. All of this continues regardless of peace initiatives.

World bodies have taken no effective action against this apartheid policy. Even the EU continues with its preferential trade agreement with Israel. UN sanctions against Israel are not even considered since Israel is a puppet of the US.

154

This is clearly one of the great injustices of the world today, perpetrated against a largely defenceless people. I raised our visit with the Minister for Foreign Affairs at a meeting of the Foreign Affairs Committee and I will continue to raise the plight of the Palestinian People at every opportunity.

He was critical of the Israeli assault on Lebanon in 2006, and made this quite clear in a speech to the Joint Committee on Foreign Affairs in the Houses of the Oireachtas, part of which appears below:

It is important that we express our condemnation, particularly of the deplorable attacks on civilians in the Lebanon.

I expressed the view at the last meeting of this committee, two weeks ago, that the killing of approximately 200 civilians constituted a war crime. Now the figure amounts to some 700 civilians and rising. It is important to repeat our condemnation of all attacks on civilians, none of which can be justified and all of which are criminal acts, no matter where or when they occur. The deliberate targeting of civilians in any war is a war crime. The problem has been that war crimes have never been addressed, except in some particular circumstances. When a state which has overwhelming military superiority uses that superiority with callous and vindictive disregard for the lives of children and the elderly its actions can only be described properly as 'war crimes' and should be responded to as such.[26]

At Tony's funeral mass, Noel went outside the prepared script to highlight in the Prayers of the Faithful the plight of the residents of Gaza then under daily bombardment by the Israelis.

Tony was also very active in opposing the Iraq War, and also spoke against it in the Dáil.

The Government has disgraced itself not only by not withdrawing over-flight and refuelling facilities at Shannon but also by not condemning the illegal unilateral action of this oil motivated war. I am not surprised that on this issue of war against the people of Iraq this Fianna Fáil led Government, just like in its social policy, is finally exposed as the most reactionary right wing political bunch in this State masquerading as a party of the centre. Young people and, indeed, most people here will be appalled to see a Government that claims to believe in an international community based on binding rules and institutions facilitate in any way a war effort that has neither international agreement or domestic support ... how long will it take before this Government will have the moral courage to stand up to Mr Bush and say that Ireland is independent; Ireland is neutral and we will have no part in this unnecessary inhumanity?[27]

NATURE, ANIMALS AND THE COUNTRYSIDE

Tony's interest and political engagement extended from geo-politics to eco-politics, or at least that part of eco-politics linked to animals. For activists in the cause of animal welfare, he was a dream partner: here was a politician who loved animals and was passionately committed to seeing them treated well. Even better, hare coursing and the like did not have a natural popular base in Dublin's north inner city and Tony was therefore immune to pressure from any of his potential voters. Indeed, if anything, his opposition to blood sports was likely to help him hoover up some additional votes among those of his electorate who shared his distaste for harm to animals. Tony opposed cruelty to animals in whatever ways it manifested itself: in neglectful or cruel conditions in the transportation of animals from place to place, or in blood sports. The two chief blood sports were hare coursing and stag hunting. Hare coursing involves pitting hares against greyhounds in confined enclosures with limited escape routes. (Inevitably, before muzzling was introduced in 1993 by the Irish Coursing Club, many hares suffered a cruel end.) The 'sport' had been banned in most other jurisdictions because of public revulsion. The second sport – stag hunting – is, strictly speaking, not a blood sport in that the hounds which chase the stag are not allowed to savage their quarry. But the reality is that the chase results in considerable trauma for the stag as it is hunted across the countryside by the hounds and the hunt members on horseback. Many stags suffer serious or fatal injury in the struggle to escape.

Tony was honoured with the office of Vice-President of the Irish Council Against Blood Sports. He was an activist on their behalf both inside and outside the Dáil. He consistently used the various mechanisms of parliamentary procedure to highlight the cause of animals and issues of cruelty. A high point in his work in this regard was his sponsorship of a Private Members Bill on wildlife in 1993. Though the Bill was defeated, it achieved a lot of publicity and revealed a good deal of political skill on Tony's part. Below are extracts from his speech making the case for the Bill in the Dáil. Bear in mind, again, that he was a lone Independent in this whole process, from negotiating parliamentary time and support to crafting his speech:

It is significant and a vindication of the democratic process that an Independent Member is enabled to move legislation in this manner. It is a particular privilege for me to present to this House a measure which, if accepted in principle in whole or in part, will advance an area of immense public concern and interest – the welfare of the vulnerable and defenceless in nature's creation. It is a measure that will hopefully help bring to an end the medieval barbarity of live hare coursing. ... I readily accept that many rural Members have come under great pressure to oppose the Bill. I know that coursing clubs can be powerful entrenched groups in many rural constituencies. I equally accept that I am not under any such pressure. What I ask – it is no small request – is that Members decide for themselves whether there is need to change this cruel practice. If they decide there is such a need, in the interests of justice I ask them not to oppose this Bill on Second Stage.

I know that this House is deeply divided on the issue of coursing. However, almost everybody is in agreement that the greyhound industry is an important traditional one which has experienced great difficulty in recent years. It is my strong view that, if the cruelty and blood lust is taken out of the industry, as has been done in so many countries worldwide, the result will be that our greyhound industry will be enhanced and, perhaps more importantly, its world reputation will undoubtedly receive the major boost it so badly needs.

[*The next day*] If this Bill is voted down tonight it will not dissuade me from pursuing this issue. I intend to take this case to the Council of Europe. The Council of Europe has stated that it will 'endeavour to ensure that animals are treated in a way that does not inflict on them any avoidable pain, suffering, distress or lasting harm'.

As a representative of Dáil Éireann on the Council of Europe, I will, along with the ISPCA and the Irish Council Against Blood Sports, pursue this matter there. I regret having to do so because I believe our reputation as a modern state will suffer significantly.[28]

On his death, the Irish Council Against Blood Sports placed a warm tribute to him on Youtube. The tribute reflected his many efforts in the cause of animal welfare over his political career.

The following Dáil speech in 2007 by Tony on the Ward Union Hunt gives a further flavour of his parliamentary work against animal cruelty and why he was so highly regarded by the animal welfare lobby. In this instance, he got double political value for his speech: he was able to target not only animal cruelty, but also to get in a dig against property developers or builders who were part of the hunt, two of whom he named. Michael Bailey was Master of the Ward Hunt which has its physical base in Dunshaughlin and draws membership from Dublin and Meath. With his brother, Tom, Michael owned Bovale Developments, a major player nationally in building and land banks. The Tribunal of Inquiry Into Certain Planning Matters and Payments, informally known as the Flood Tribunal after its sole member Mr Justice Feargus Flood, investigated, among many other things, aspects of Michael Bailey's relationship with Fianna Fáil politician and Minister Ray Burke. In its second interim report, Chapter 18, paragraph 9, the Tribunal found that Ray Burke had received 'a corrupt payment' from Bailey. Ray Burke subsequently received a jail sentence. Johnny Ronan, another member of the hunt, cultivated a high-profile lifestyle and enjoyed more media attention than many of his fellow property developers. In 1989, with Richard Barrett, Ronan founded Treasury Holdings. The Treasury Holdings Group became a significant player in property development in Europe and Asia, with a strong presence in Dublin, London and Shanghai. Parts of his property empire are now part of the NAMA process.

> I have been present to monitor the activities of the Ward Union Hunt and witnessed Mr Bailey, Mr Ronan and others like them at their entertainment. In terror of the hounds, the deer frantically tries to stay in front of them but, being in unfamiliar territory, the route is hazardous and it crashes through hedges, jumps over walls and ditches, crosses busy roads and even runs down busy streets. It is a gruelling ordeal which can last for up to three hours and result in tears, bruises, bites, lameness and exhaustion.

> Veterinary documents obtained by the Irish Council Against Blood Sports under the Freedom of Information Act have exposed some of the fatalities arising from the Ward Union Hunt's activities, including a deer which died as a result of fractured ribs, two deer which died from ruptured aortic aneurysms, a deer which drowned in a quarry and a deer which collapsed and died after desperately trying to escape over an 8ft high wall. When the animal becomes so depleted it can no longer run, hunt members move in to tackle it violently to the ground.[29]

ANGLO-IRISH BANK AND THE DUBLIN DOCKLANDS

Tony was well ahead of the game in spotting crucial conflicts of interest in the membership of the Board of the Docklands Authority which had been mandated to promote the development of a twenty-seven acre site previously owned by the Dublin Port and Docks Board. In a failure to grasp the issue, or a concerted attempt to mask it, either of which proved to have epic implications, the then Fianna Fáil Minister for the Environment Dick Roche tried to pooh-pooh Tony's concern, which Tony expressed in the form of a Dáil question on 4 November 2004. This was a local issue with national implications and that was how Tony saw most of his political agenda as a Dáil deputy: the problems of the inner city were merely symptoms of a wider malaise. How true in the case of the financial services sector.

In an exchange between them in the Dáil, Tony argued his case.[30]

Mr Gregory: This executive board is effectively the planning authority for the docklands area. Some of the board members, including the chairman, are associated with Anglo Irish Bank, which is now funding the largest development in the whole north docklands, a development to which they, as board members, granted the planning permission in the first place. The Minister referred to a code of conduct in his reply. What course of action will the board's code of conduct provide when these same developers make new planning applications and come to the docklands board looking for planning permission? Will members associated with Anglo Irish Bank, including the chairman, simply absent themselves and if so, how could the board of the DDDA realistically fulfil its functions as planning authority in those circumstances? On the other hand, if they do not absent themselves, there must surely be a question of a conflict of interest when they are making a decision on future planning applications.

How are local community interests protected in this set up? Is it any wonder a local residents' leader expressed serious concerns regarding the Spencer Dock development, where planning permission was granted in contravention of the docklands own master plan while the views of the community representatives on the docklands' council were ignored? Following that–

An Ceann Comhairle: A question, please, Deputy.

Mr Gregory: I am concluding the question, Cheann Comhairle. The bank with which some board members are associated funds the Spencer Dock

development and the chairman of the authority accepts a position on the board of that bank. The Minister must surely agree that a very serious conflict of interest exists somewhere. I ask the Minister whether it is time to review the membership of the Dublin Docklands Development Authority.

Mr Roche: I thank the Deputy for those questions. I reiterate the point that in a relatively small city in European terms, it is very difficult to find people willing to–

Mr Gregory: I have specific questions.

Mr Roche: I listened with courtesy to the Deputy and I ask him to do the same. I will answer the specific points raised by the Deputy. The board operates as a planning authority and the point I made is none the less valid in that regard because the membership of the board is drawn from a relatively narrow pool. Planning decisions are taken by the executive board of the DDDA. They have regard to the assessment and to the recommendations of the professional staff. As with all other planning issues, those are recommendations. Possible conflicts of interest will inevitably arise from time to time but if the Deputy is suggesting that they have behaved with impropriety, then that is a very serious allegation.

Tony's concern was to prove prophetic in the epic collapse of the Irish banking system from late 2009. Especially notable was the collapse of Anglo Irish Bank whose senior leadership were closely entwined in the membership of the Docklands Authority. Minister Roche chose not to engage with the issues which Tony was raising. In due course, the electorate of the Wicklow constituency which Minister Roche represented exacted their price for his part in the Fianna Fáil government's failure to protect the public interest, when, with many Fianna Fáil colleagues, he was unseated in the 2011 general election.

THE TECHNICAL GROUP

An achievement Tony greatly valued was forming and leading the Technical Group in Dáil Éireann in the period 2002 to 2007. He saw this as demonstrating what Independents could achieve by working together. As a clear sign of the meaning he attached to its work and his role, he wanted a mention of this at his funeral.

Forming the Technical Group was a tactical move by Tony and his associates. Tony was very much the driving force. The Technical Group was essentially an ad hoc political grouping formed for the purpose of acquiring certain rights that political parties of a minimum size automatically gain. The right to parliamentary time to make speeches and to put down motions for debate are closely guarded by the government and the main political parties. This puts isolated Independents on the back foot. For most of his time in the Dáil, Tony found himself in this marginal position, wheedling scraps of speaking time from other parties so that he could have some say in debates. The two periods when he got more 'air time' were in the short eight-month period of the Haughey-led government in 1982, and in the period of the Technical Group (2002-07). He had enjoyed a special status initially since his vote, via the Gregory Deal, had been critical in electing and maintaining the government. The electoral arithmetic never again fell quite so favourably for Tony although in 2002 the number of Independents elected was sufficient to allow them to form the Technical Group. During the tributes in the Dáil after Tony's death, Finian McGrath recalled his critical role in the formation of the Technical Group: 'Tony was the brains behind the formation of the Technical Group and was very protective and defensive of it.[31]'

Tony conceived the idea of the group and was willing to mentor the other members in their political development as TDs, many of them being newly elected. He enjoyed being Chief Whip of the Technical Group, something he proudly proclaimed on his personal Dáil notepaper. The role meant

that he determined parliamentary strategy for the group. It meant that he
had a lot of contact, as their peer, with the Chief Whips of the political
parties, an opportunity which he enjoyed and exploited. In this way he
managed, for example, to secure agreement to an adjournment debate on
further education.[32]

All through his years in the Dáil, Tony spoke out for causes he supported
and used many parliamentary devices and gestures to highlight issues, including the Technical Group, making innumerable speeches, presenting endless
oral and written questions and sponsoring a high-profile Private Members
Bill on animal welfare.

LIFE AS A COUNCILLOR

While very proud to be a TD, Tony also took his work as a councillor
very seriously. Being a Dáil deputy did not mean losing touch with local
issues and local controversies in Dublin City Council. He was still careful to
remain exposed to local opinion and concerns. While generally there was
a good fit between his instincts and local wishes, Tony sometimes found he
had to assert his views in the face of some local opposition. One example
arose in 1985, when Tony secured the unanimous support of his fellow city
councillors for his proposal to name the bridge over the River Tolka at Ballybough after Luke Kelly soon after the singer's death. Luke was an iconic
figure in Dublin life, a much-loved member of The Dubliners, the hugely
popular folk group. Luke had been born in Sheriff Street and this inner-city
connection provided much of the impetus for the idea of re-naming the
bridge. But the idea got up the nose of some locals. There were some objections, which today sound rather po-faced. The complainants argued that
Kelly's 'status as a ballad singer and his liking for a pint of Guinness were not
sufficient qualities to warrant a bridge being named after him.'[33] Perhaps the
opponents disliked being associated with someone from 'Sheriffer', the local

nickname for Sheriff Street. But the protests did not win out. Tony and the other councillors held firm. Tony, for once, chose to ignore local opinion, or a certain slice thereof. The bridge was opened with its new name on 30 May 1985 by the Lord Mayor, Jim Tunney (known as the 'Yellow Rose of Finglas' among his constituents, after the trademark yellow rose in his lapel). Like most serious politicians, Tony thrived at 'occasions', and with various notables in attendance, including Charlie Haughey, by now the leader of the opposition, Jim Tunney TD as Lord Mayor and Labour TD, Michael D Higgins, the poet, sociologist and man never lost for words, Tony had indeed created a fitting occasion in honour of Luke.[34] All that was needed was a song from the much-missed man himself.

Tony was not afraid to stand alone in pursuit of his political goals on the Council. But he also had a natural affinity with Christy Burke, the Provisional Sinn Féin councillor, first elected in 1985 and a representative of the inner city for many years, as they agreed on a lot of issues. Christy recalls how the political establishment sought to freeze him out of Council business in these pre-Peace Process days when representatives of the political wing of the republican movement were treated as pariahs in punishment for their association with the IRA and its campaign of violence in the North. This was before the Hume–Adams talks, which commenced in 1988 and the idea that the road to peace might require generosity and imagination on both sides. Like any councillor, Christy could make proposals only if he had a seconder for the motion – and the only fellow-councillor willing to serve as a seconder for him was Tony.[35] This experience presumably helped lay the foundation of their political friendship over the years, but Tony's stance on this was not just about friendship, it also foreshadowed both his oft-expressed wish for collaboration among Left-minded politicians and the ultimate success of the technical group in the period 2002-07 in the Dáil. And, of course, helping Burke in this way also reflected Tony's quiet loyalty to his republican roots.

Tony also played an important part in helping to modernise the institution of Dublin Corporation which, in terms of policy and approach to citizens and councillors, was fairly antiquated at the time he first joined the Council. The reforms he sought were pretty run of the mill by international standards of good local governance. What had been radical under the '*ancien regime*' which ended with the retirement of Frank Feeley, just seemed like mainstream common sense under the highly competent, technocratic and inclusive leadership of John Fitzgerald. The arrival of John Fitzgerald as City Manager in June 1996, and his transformational approach, highlighted how much reform in governance was both needed and possible. Not all of Fitzgerald's reforms would necessarily have won favour with Tony, but here at least was a manager with a refreshingly energetic, inclusive, innovative, 'can do' and problem-solving approach. He also had a perspective that resonated, at least in part, with some of the original demands of NCCC. He peppered his policy approach with phrases such as 'bottom-up' and 'local partnership'. Crucially, he moved key chunks of city administration out of central offices to local areas so that decision-makers were closer to the areas affected by their decisions.

TONY'S RELATIONS WITH THE CHURCH

It's probably true to say that I had an excess of religion in the first twenty years of my life and I just haven't been able to cope with any more since! When I was growing up, my mother was hugely religious – as country women, in particular, were. My mother had an intense devotion to the Blessed Virgin and all the traditions of the Catholic faith. I went to the 'Nine First Fridays' as they called the 8 o'clock mass. I ended up going to 8 o'clock mass every day of the week. I was an altar boy. I was a member of the Legion of Mary. I wouldn't be anti-religious in any way. I respect people's beliefs and so on.[36]

Tony, the adult, had become disillusioned with the institutional Church and admitted that his childhood faith had faded – in spite of this he maintained his mother's habit of saving used stamps to send to the Medical Missionaries of Mary for their fund-raising! As a politician, he had also been critical of the Church for its part as an education provider in the decline of educational provision for local people in the inner city. It is also pretty clear that certain interests in the Church in the inner city were hostile to his political role in the early days – but that did not last. While he might have been skeptical of the institutions, he respected some individual priests within the Church who shared his commitment to improving conditions in the inner city. The choice of Peter McVerry to deliver the homily at Tony's funeral mass was a strong signal of the esteem in which the Jesuit was held by Tony. McVerry is a tireless campaigner for homeless youth, and works at the frontline of care provision, and raising public awareness and support. Peter had spent six years from 1974 living in a flat in the block of tenements along the notorious Summerhill, before they were torn down in the process of redevelopment of parts of the north inner city. This had been a transforming experience for McVerry personally and altered the course of his work subsequently. [37]

The final *coup de grace* for Summerhill had been the decision of the Corporation, in its infinite wisdom, to use the block as a dumping ground for rent defaulters from across the city. Concentrating families with the wider difficulties inevitably associated with rent defaulting had perfectly predictable consequences. The fact that it was considered suitable as a punishment zone was also a sign of the condition to which the place had been allowed to descend.

Another priest who had connections with Tony was Fr Michael Casey, the tall and popular Kerry man who served both as curate and later as parish priest in Sean McDermott Street parish for eight years from 1978 to 1986. Mick had a wonderful way with him that won over many who were not normally drawn to churchmen. His smile and good humour were infectious. And his addiction to coaching basketball went down well in a community that liked its sport. Casey acted as a *de facto* spokesman for Tony while he was in prison with Christy Burke on the street traders issue, and is reported to have spent every evening on the demonstration outside Mountjoy – this role may not have been formally organised, but it reflected the close liaison and mutual respect between the two men. Another priest who earned Tony's respect was the Salesian Fr Joe Lucey, who had run various youth projects in the inner city over a fifteen-year period. Tony spoke in the Dáil of his contribution on the occasion of his death:

> I take the opportunity ... to pay tribute to the late Fr Joe Lucey who did magnificent work – I am not overstating it in any way. Our Lady of Lourdes Church on Sean MacDermott Street was packed last night as a tribute to his work. He is certainly an immense loss to that community in the north inner city and to the marginalised young people in the Crinan Youth Project and in other projects with which he worked over the years.[38]

Among the VIPs at Tony's own funeral was the Catholic Archbishop of Dublin, Diarmuid Martin. His presence marked formal recognition of Tony's contribution to the city, but in an interestingly understated way: the Archbishop remained in the congregation rather than taking a place on the altar as Church dignitaries might have done in the past. If Church worthies had to adjust in the midst of the funeral service, so also did many of Tony's political associates on the Left, who were stunned by his choice of a religious service, given their own emotional preference for a more secular event. Tony's choice seems to have had a complex motivation, but was linked in a significant way to the influence of his mother, in the estimation of Maureen O'Sullivan – she also thinks Tony's choice was out of a loyalty to so many of his voters who would be more comfortable with the familiarity of a Church funeral. Reflecting on his choice of funeral service, Philip Boyd observed that he felt that Tony was 'an agnostic rather than a convinced atheist'.

TONY'S CRITICS AND OPPONENTS

While he may have won admiration across the political spectrum, even from those who might not have been natural fans of his mix of community politics, socialism and republicanism, there were others who remained antagonistic. There were critics of the original Gregory Deal – most vocal at the time was Fine Gael TD Gay Mitchell. There were also critics railing against any attempt to resurrect such an arrangement to secure Gregory's support in later critical Dáil votes, although Tony proved well able to defend his corner.

Garret FitzGerald revived the issue of the merits of the Gregory Deal in 2000 when, eighteen years after the Deal, he wrote a piece lamenting what he saw as a drift towards localism in Irish politics. He claimed the Gregory Deal reached by Haughey had been the catalyst and precedent for this trend.[39] FitzGerald was making a reasonable point about the abuse of ministerial office in the context of decisions about locations in relation to the decentralisation of the public and civil service, a disastrous and ill-thought out policy visited on the country by Charlie McCreevy, Fianna Fáil Finance Minister (1997–2004) who, of course, also played no small part in cultivating the excesses of the Celtic Tiger economy, with his calamitous mantra of 'light touch financial regulation'. But attributing the source of responsibility for this tendency for misguided localism to the Gregory Deal was stretching things too far. In placing the blame on the Gregory Deal, Garret was conveniently, for the sake of his own argument, overlooking the reality that localism was historically embedded in Irish political culture long before the Gregory Deal, a point highlighted many years previously by Basil Chubb, the one-time Trinity political science professor and popular RTÉ television pundit for elections from the 1960s to the 1980s. Chubb mentioned this in his classic book of its time, *Government and Politics in Ireland*, where he argued that in an election 'the candidate's best asset by far is his record of service in the home district'.[40] The implication of Chubb's point was that candidates

Top: Tony greets Palestinian leader Yasser Arafat, with Lord Mayor of Dublin, Tomás Mac Giolla.

Above: Tony meets Cuban leader Fidel Castro in Cuba at the 105th Inter-Parliamentary Conference in Havana, 2001. Tony was not scheduled to meet Castro as he was not the leader of the national delegation, but, wanting to fulfil a lifelong ambition, he slipped quietly into the waiting line. (*Source: Gregory family*)

Tony's involvement in animal rights issues: (*left*) as a TD at a Compassion in World Farming press conference, May 1999 (*Source: R. Coe*); (*below*) at an Irish Council Against Blood Sports protest.

Opposite: Tony attends a dramatic anti-drugs protest meeting in his constituency, 22 August 1996.
(*Source: Derek Speirs*).

Above: Councillor Tony Gregory meets Mother Teresa in the Mansion House, Dublin, on the occasion of her receiving the Freedom of the City. Also in the picture are Cardinal Desmond Connell (left), Lord Mayor Gay Mitchell (centre) and Councillor Sean Haughey (right).

Below: Postering for the 2007 election near Belvedere Road, North Circular Road; even late in his career Tony clambered up poles to get his message across! (*Source: Maxwells*)

Above: Tony holds an injured racing pigeon he rescued in Wexford and brought home for recovery, 2006. (*Source: Annette Dolan*)

Below: Tony relaxing on holidays with his partner of his later years, Annette Dolan. (*Source: Annette Dolan*)

Above: Tony at the anti-Iraq War Demonstration in Dublin 2003, with Finian McGrath TD (left) and Senator David Norris (right).

Left: Tony greets US President Bill Clinton, with Taoiseach Bertie Ahern, December 2000.

Above: The first 'Technical Group' of independent TDs, 2002 to 2007, outside Leinster House. The formation of this group was a major achievement for Independents. Tony was the Chief Whip and Joe Higgins was leader of the group.

(*Front row, left to right*) Catherine Murphy, Tony Gregory, Marian Harkin, Jerry Cowley.

(*Back row, left to right*) Paudge Connolly, James Breen, Paddy McHugh, Joe Higgins, Finian McGrath. (*Source: Kevin Carr Photography*)

Below: Tony with his beloved dog at the canal bank in Ballybough where they often walked. (*Source: Steve Humphries, Irish Independent*)

Above: An announcement from the Irish Campaign Against Blood Sports on the death of Tony Gregory.

Left: Tony Gregory's legacy continues – Maureen O'Sullivan, his friend and supporter for many years, was elected on the 'Gregory ticket' to Dáil Éireann in 2009.

tended to see local issues as more important than national ones. So localism in Irish politics was certainly not something cooked up by Haughey and Gregory from scratch in the course of their deal. In his skilful rejection of FitzGerald's argument, Tony pointed out that the deal was entirely in the public domain and many of the issues in it were national rather than local in character.[41] In support of his point, he quoted the assessment of the Gregory Deal by the highly regarded Irish historian, Joseph Lee:

> **Critics denounced the idea of a special deal as disgraceful, allegedly debasing the political coinage. What was disgraceful in this case was less the deal than the fact that it needed a deal to win some attention for one of the most deprived areas of the country, an inner city constituency ravaged by poverty and neglect, and their concomitants, unemployment, bad housing and a vicious drugs problem.[42]**

In his autobiography, Bertie Ahern indulged in what seems like some subtle 'revisionism' in relation to events involving Tony, while also (of course!) professing admiration for Tony's success. Ahern tried to claim that Haughey had liaised closely with him (Ahern) during the process leading up to the Deal and indeed that Ahern himself had orchestrated some of the preparations on the government side. But the picture may not be so clear. Certainly Martin Mansergh made no mention of Ahern's role in an interview he did with Vincent Browne reviewing his then twenty years' work in the Department of the Taoiseach.[43] Mansergh had helped to brief Haughey in the Deal negotiations. Tony says that Bertie gave Haughey a lift to Summerhill.[44] The interesting point here is Ahern is the only survivor – the other principals (Haughey and Gregory) are not alive to confirm or deny what he is claiming. Ahern also asserts that Tony had come from the IRSP into community politics. There may be some political sleight of hand here: it implies a much greater level of involvement in the IRSP than seems actually to have been the case. Tony's own version, as set out in his *Hot Press* interview, is that he was never active in the party as he had grown disillusioned with parties after his experience in Official Sinn Féin where initially he had given of himself wholeheartedly. He had joined the IRSP reluctantly at the express request of his hero Seamus Costello. Insofar as he was active to any degree on that front, it seems that his loyalty was personal to Costello rather than to the party as such. Any connection to the IRSP certainly ceased on the death of Costello. There had been a considerable interval, including a brief dalliance with the Socialist Labour Party, before Tony began to emerge as a force in the new community politics in the north inner city that he helped to fashion.

The Sinn Féin The Workers Party seemed to resent Tony's electoral success, which in many instances was in contrast to their own performance. Their magazine, *The Workers' Life*, took a critical line on the Deal, alleging that Gregory had 'turned his back on true socialism … and [had pursued] parish pump politics in an urban setting … on a lavish scale.'[45] As Brian Hanley and Scott Millar note, this criticism was made despite the fact that the SFWP TDs had also voted for the election of Haughey as Taoiseach!

There are also some who had reservations about Tony's naming of drug barons in the Dáil. However well intentioned his motives for doing so, this still represents, according to this viewpoint, a dangerous precedent and a major infringement of the civil rights of individuals and a threat to their safety by people who might take this as a signal to take matters into their own hands. From the vantage point of those communities and individuals suffering at the hands of drug crime, however, it must be said that this may seem like a fine and abstract theological point far removed from the brutal realities of life in communities crushed by drug crime.

While Tony grew to be liked by people across the political spectrum, he still had his critics, some of whom did not recognise his independence of thought. Tony's brother, Noel, recalls the journalist and commentator Eoghan Harris making a rather harsh comment around the peak of Tony's engagement with blood sports issues, along the lines of: how come Tony could be so opposed to the killing of animals in the South when he didn't oppose the killing of humans, who happened to be Protestants, in the North? More than twenty years later, Noel's anger against what he sees as the injustice of this comment is undimmed: 'We had Protestant blood from both parents' families. Our grandfather on our father's side converted to Catholicism to marry our grandmother. In no way did Tony support sectarian violence.'

REGRETS

One political regret that Tony admitted to was not having the opportunity to hold a post of Junior Minister (or Super Junior Minister attending Cabinet) with a brief for an area in which he had expertise, such as drugs or inner-city development. Yet the reality is that Tony actually had a higher profile and a stronger track record of impact than most junior ministers could ever hope to achieve. It is pretty safe to say that no Junior Minister to date can look back on a record of specific political achievements that comes close to Tony's. It is all the more remarkable that he achieved these gains from the backbenches as an Independent, and almost always while in opposition. There was strong speculation that he might have accepted the office of Ceann Comhairle – the presiding officer of the Dáil – if it had been offered in the summer of 1997, as the new government sought to nail down the basis of a working majority.[46] But this proved not to be.

Another regret of Tony's was not to have served as Lord Mayor of his native city. David Norris saw him as 'a proud Dubliner, someone who loved his city'. It is safe to say that he is probably the best Lord Mayor that Dublin never had. He came close to being elected Lord Mayor in 1998, and claimed that Fianna Fáil reneged on a deal, thanks to the intervention of Bertie Ahern, who obviously did not want this added profile for Tony for his own constituency reasons.[47] Curiously, Tony shares this dubious status of never being Lord Mayor with another long-serving Dublin politician,

Charles Haughey, who also began his career as a city councillor but also never became Lord Mayor of his native city.[48]

Asked if he was disappointed that he did not get the Ceann Comhairle post, whether he had been 'crushed by the rebuff', he responded: 'If I'm crushed by anything, it's that by virtue of my independence I've been excluded from any position of influence all my political life.'[49]

Those words, twelve years before his death, and well into his political career, betray feelings of bitterness and frustration that he did not reveal in public very often. Even his opponents would have to concede that Tony was extremely able. This ability, combined with a huge appetite for hard work and detail, made him a formidable political operator. He must have been frustrated at times to see many other politicians who demonstrated less ability or less hard work achieving more recognition for less performance. The fact that he was excluded from *formal* positions of influence might be said to be a back-handed compliment. It seems that he was seen as being too able to be allowed into the tent in a formal way. His values, appeal and intelligence might have been seen as making him too big a force to contain.

But any fair reading of Tony's achievements would have to allow that Tony sometimes underestimated the influence he carved out *informally* through community initiatives in relation to drugs, youth, policing and much more. It is also the case that Tony started off in politics as the quintessential out-sider, and right through his career that remained a card he could play to his political advantage. Being kept out of office also meant never having to take the rap for unpopular policies.

Tony was a critic of the status quo, but he was not satisfied with words alone. He wanted action, he was fundamentally an activist — a 'doer'. He wanted to find ways of doing things better, of getting things done more effectively. He may not have been recognised widely for this, but he was truly an innovator. At a time now when the institutions of state and business are in disarray and proving unequal to the demands of what is necessary, it is clear that Tony's views and urges are being vindicated. In his sphere of activity, he could see the need for institutional reform in how policing was conducted, in relations between local government and local communities, in the relations between State institutions and ordinary citizens, in how the education system faced up to the realities of its own failures. Tony believed in honesty and accountability. He believed in telling it as it was. He believed in demanding a response from those in authority that engaged with that reality, and not with some bogus version of reality that better suited their short-term purpose. He was intelligent, he was hard-working, he was committed – and he knew what he was talking about. He was a very rare bird. He was also a politician with a deep and sustained interest in poverty and disadvantage. And he was a politician with first-hand experience of poverty and disadvantage in his own upbringing and in his daily encounters in his constituency.

While he operated without a party, he did manage to assemble an inner core of supporters who proved important to his success – Fergus McCabe and Mick Rafferty made up with Tony a key trio, but there were others too who were important over the long haul, not least Maureen O'Sullivan, as well, of course, as Tony's brother, Noel. They all worked hard but also thrived on the fun and humour that inevitably were part of proceedings in Dublin and its overlapping networks. In a delicious example of this, and of how small a village Dublin can sometimes be, Fergus found himself at a retirement 'do' for a senior Garda in his current role as a respected community organiser (and member of the local Community Policing Forum). The event was to mark the retirement from the force of the Assistant Commissioner of the Garda Síochána for Dublin, Al McHugh, the most senior-ranking Garda in Dublin. Over a glass of wine, McHugh enquired quietly of Fergus whether he had lived in Kinvara Park years ago? When Fergus confirmed this, McHugh somewhat sheepishly admitted that he had been the officer who had arrested Fergus at the street protest for which he was imprisoned thirty years earlier.

While broadly there was remarkable harmony between the three principals in the Gregory camp over the years, there were inevitably some bumps on the road. Fergus took the idea of giving a voice to local people very seriously. On one occasion, Tony had written an excoriating piece in the local *Inner City News* on the political failings of Michael O'Leary, a local TD at the time and one-time leader of the Labour Party – before his departure to Fine Gael. Though Fergus found himself agreeing with much of the content, he also found himself consoling an aggrieved Maureen Grant, a resident in the Summerhill tenement block and a long-standing Labour Party supporter, who for her 'day job' worked as a much-loved manager of the bar at night in the Olympia Theatre. True to his belief of giving voice to locals even if he didn't necessarily share all their views, Fergus helped Maureen to draft a riposte to Tony's damning critique of O'Leary. Needless to remark, Tony was not very impressed with Fergus's generosity in this instance.

One of the keys to their success was the fact that Tony, Mick and Fergus understood, crucially, that development was about *people* – not just about physical buildings or infrastructure, and not just about collective action. Real change also happened one person at a time. The story of Councillor Marie Metcalfe illustrates this point well. Marie's mother was active in community work in her area, and as a youngster Marie used to tag along to meetings, and then to hang out in the offices of NCCCAP. She remembers first meeting Tony, Fergus and Mick when she was twelve years old; she thought the three of them were 'hippies – with their long hair and lots to say'. She recalls having great fun as a teenager being around the action and soaking up the atmosphere. It was a remarkable way to serve what proved to be an apprenticeship as a community activist. Marie remembers running a week-long summer project for children in North Clarence Street flats, with her friend Sheila Leech, when they were both around sixteen years of age. It was a great success. The week culminated in a performance by a live band. She still thinks of it as 'the best week of my life'. So impressed were the older activists on the committee with the success of the week that they found the money to send the two sixteen-year-olds – Marie and her pal – off for a weekend. Tony became a fixture in Marie's life, attending her twenty-first birthday party, her wedding, her daughter's christening, her grand-daughter's christening. By some mix-up, Tony wasn't told about a surprise party for her fortieth, and he was not impressed. Marie is now a city councillor, holding Tony's old Council seat. She took pleasure in being addressed as 'Councillor Metcalfe' on her first visit to the City Council offices, after her nomination, in Tony's place, as a Councillor. 'It was only two years earlier that I had signed for my gaff [rented City Council flat] in the same offices!' She thoroughly enjoys the status of being the only serving councillor who is also a tenant of the Council. Marie has also played a major part in the community policing initiative in the north inner city. Still scarcely believing he is dead, Marie Metcalf says of Tony, 'He always made me feel I could do it … I am who I am because of Tony and Fergus – they had a major influence on my life.'

Tony's legacy lies not so much in the achievement of high office or a list of legislative reform. In many ways, his legacy is more important and more enduring: with his political voice he changed, forever, perceptions outsiders held of the inner city of Dublin, and of its people and its issues. Even more importantly, his voice helped to change forever how local people in the inner city saw themselves, their issues and their own power and influence.

CHAPTER 8

• • • • • •

The Private Side

Towards the end of my first interview about Tony with Noel, he said to me quite spontaneously, that Tony was 'silent, shy and private as a small boy' and that as an adult he 'was still very private as a politician'. These qualities are also much commented on by others with whom I spoke. These views chimed with my own experience of contact with Tony. He was not someone who found it easy to open up, or more precisely he was very selective about the occasions and people involved when he did. There were various views as to the reasons for Tony's characteristic reticence. There was some speculation that it arose from the discipline instilled from his time in the republican movement. It is also possible that he grew up with older parents from a generation that was frugal not just in minding money, but also in 'minding their own business' – and frugality is a pretty close relative of self-reliance and reticence.

Tony could display a formidable exterior when required, but this did not represent the whole Tony. There was a gentler side. Animals in need could bring out the softie in him. Annette Dolan, his partner in his later years, recalls his bringing an injured bird home from Wexford: he packaged the bird carefully in a box and placed it in the boot of the car, and somehow the bird survived the journey so that proper care and rehabilitation could be arranged.

But Tony was certainly not ruled by frugality in his adult life. He enjoyed companionship and good company. He was a hard worker but not a complete workaholic. He could relax, he enjoyed the outdoors, a good meal, foreign travel. He had had a girlfriend in his days in UCD, a romance to which he referred in a number of interviews – its ending still clearly hurt years later. There were further romantic commitments with a number of women along the way and those relationships certainly helped him to find a life beyond politics. Not that politics was ever far away in Tony's life.

He liked his glass of wine, but generally did not drink to excess. He especially enjoyed Christmas parties involving those in the wider network of community projects which he supported. Fergus McCabe recalls Tony wending his way home in very good form from a Christmas outing to a restaurant off Grafton Street. Passing the Molly Malone statue, Tony felt the urge to climb onto the plinth to deliver a speech to the good citizens of Dublin; unfortunately, he lost his balance and fell into the bushes surrounding the city's annual Christmas tree at the bottom of Grafton Street. The sight of a well-known politician crawling out of the greenery must have caused some puzzlement for passers by.

Tony could appreciate the finer things in life. David Norris recalls how much Tony celebrated the great craftsmanship in the houses of Georgian Dublin, despite the fact that Georgian Dublin had originated with a different social class' Tony had a fund of great stories. He enjoyed foreign travel as a parliamentarian. But he was still marked by his upbringing in the inner city. As Maureen O'Sullivan puts it, 'He still knew where the real world was.' He found it hard to shake off all the traces of the frugality of his early life, but while he may have been careful with money, he was generous with his time. John Lynch, his friend from primary school days, and later from UCD, recalls being hospitalised for an extended period in his early twenties, and Tony being very assiduous in visiting him almost every day. This spirit of generosity also came to be a hallmark of the way the group around him operated in community politics. They were extraordinarily helpful, as Pauline Kane recalls. She was a very young office worker in the early days of the NCCCAP, and she recalls someone fishing out an old typewriter from somewhere to help her to hone her fledgling typing skills as a new recruit; then the day it appeared, she remembers Mick Rafferty saying to her, 'I'm passing your door, I'll give you and that typewriter a lift.' Next thing, Mick was carrying the typewriter up the stairs to Pauline's family flat on the upper levels of Avondale House in Cumberland Street. (Pauline was the person who later typed the Deal document.) Reflecting on Tony's political contribution, Pauline says that political integrity was another quality that people valued in Tony. He didn't lead people on with what they wanted to hear. His fundamental honesty always shone through. He always named it as it was. And sometimes that meant close associates getting it between the eyes if he felt they merited it.

The inner – and wider – circle of Tony's supporters were bonded by shared concerns to improve the lot of inner-city residents young and old, and by a conviction that Tony had the ability and commitment to make an impact. Many supporters were drawn to Tony by his personal charisma and absolute honesty.[1]

Liz Doyle knew Tony from his early days in Sinn Féin. Liz and her mother stayed in touch socially with some of the people who shared their political connections over the years. Tony turned up now and again for a chat at some of these social gatherings, and his yarns and wit were always in demand. Tony got on well with Liz's mother, who was very fond of him, and Liz remembers warmly Tony's kindness when her mother died. Tony spent a lot of time with the family in the period between Mrs Doyle's death and her burial, a couple of days later. His generosity with his time at that point made a big impression on Liz.

Although he kept it under wraps much of the time, Tony also had a good sense of humour which found expression in the right circumstances. David Norris recalls how much Tony enjoyed playing parts in various Bloomsday scenes commemorating Joyce's fictional day in *Ulysses*. These were played out against the backdrop of the north inner city. Norris recalls the performances by Tony and Mick Rafferty as being 'hilarious'. Yet this humour wasn't a strong part of the public persona he presented to his wider elector-ate. An interview about the importance of pet dogs in his life gave a rare and gentle glimpse of his sense of humour, the topic helping him, perhaps, to relax his guard: 'Over the years Chilly has been great company. Politics can be a lonely world, especially, if you're an Independent. Myself and Chilly have had many powerful political conversations. And, you know what, in the end, I'm always right. That's what I like about dogs. They're consistent.'[2]

He could also enjoy a joke at his own expense – up to a point. Finian McGrath recalled his response to some of the ribbing they used to get from journalist Sam Smyth over the Technical Group of which they were both members in the Dáil from 2002-07: 'We used to see that look or dry smile on his face anytime Sam Smyth joked about people in the group, especially with remarks like: "They'd be a great crowd to fix your car." Tony enjoyed that kind of wit, but if anyone crossed the line, they were finished and they got that look again.'[3]

In the words of Maureen O'Sullivan at his funeral mass, 'He was no saint – we loved him, but there were times when we could kill him because he could be so exasperating, grumpy and, of course, he was always right.' Mau-reen conceded that 'Tony the politician didn't do much smiling, but Tony, the private person, the friend did. He had a great sense of humour, he was great company, a great teller of stories ...' Even his political opponents had a glimpse of these sides of Tony. At the first meeting after his death of the Dáil Committee on Foreign Affairs, of which Tony had been a long-standing member, Dr Michael Woods, as Chair, offered sympathy and a brief tribute in which he said that he 'always found him to be honest, courteous, hard-working and witty'. These words from Woods might be said to have meant something since there seemed to be little in his background that suggested any affinity with Tony's take on the world.

It seems safe to say that Tony did not treat the Dáil as a club. According to some accounts he was not that close to many people there. Yet, he made some connections and these did not always follow predictable ideological fault lines. Regular lunch mates were Shane Ross, a stockbroker, a financial journalist, a thorn in the side of the financial establishment, an Independent senator elected by the Trinity College graduates, (and from 2011 an Independent TD with a former leaning towards Fine Gael) and Sam Smyth, from the North of Ireland, a very experienced political journalist with a wonderful sense of humour and a great appetite for Tony's latest 'war stories' from the front line of the inner city. In the Dáil, Tony warmed to people who knew where they stood politically. He liked people who were true to their own political beliefs, irrespective of whether Tony actually shared those beliefs.[4]

In his everyday dealings with people, Tony generally gave the impression of being shy and reserved. But there was a slightly more daredevil side to him, as Fergus McCabe recalls. At one point Tony owned a souped-up blue Ford Capri 1600cc that had elegant, sporty lines – and he thoroughly enjoyed getting the most out of the car in terms of speed. On one occasion, he was caught well over the speed limit in County Clare – this was in the days before he was an elected politician but was already a community activist. Tony figured that he should have a character witness to sing his praises to the court, in the hope that this might dissuade the court from applying too severe a sanction that might damage any political aspirations. He enlisted Fergus to regale the court with the wonders of Tony's contribution to the quality of life in the inner city of Dublin. Fergus ruefully recalls sitting terrified as Tony's passenger on the way to the court hearing. The irony was not lost on Fergus of Tony speeding to the court hearing and Fergus witnessing his driving well in excess of the speed limits in advance of Fergus taking the stand to extol Tony's general virtues as a good citizen. In the same vein, Philip Boyd claims that on one occasion Tim (Tiger) O'Brien, a gentle but formidably built man with a nickname of purpose, was so terrified in the front seat with Tony's speeding that the shape of his fingertips was indented in the dashboard when the car came skidding to a halt. Tony was regularly on the roster for giving lifts to inner-city youth groups heading off on holidays or weekends away. Fergus recalls that Tony's car was very popular with the young people – there was high demand to travel with Tony because of his taste for speed. Pat Carthy also recalls an incident when Tony, with a car load of passengers, misjudged a bend at speed in County Cavan near the Cavan Centre of which Tony was a director. The Capri and all on board crashed through a hedge and sailed through the air, coming to a thudding halt twenty feet below. The car somehow landed 'on all fours' and the chastened passengers clambered out, counting their blessings that there had been no trees or rocks in their path. Tony, meanwhile, was preoccupied only with the fact that he had damaged his 'spots' – the spot-lamps beloved of serious car 'heads'. The offending bend became known to those on the inside track as 'Gregory's Hatch'. Tony's reputation as a speedster grew to the point that those in the know avoided being his passenger – once bitten, twice shy.

Tony was very competitive – even on two wheels. There was a sponsored 55-mile cycle from Dublin to Kilnacrott in Cavan each year from 1981 to raise funds for what eventually became known as the Cavan Centre. Tony took part every year and always came first. Some of the other cyclists came on fancy racing bikes and were kitted out in the latest professional cycling regalia, but Tony was in his ordinary gear and rode the plain bike he used around his constituency. But he was a good cyclist, he was fit and he didn't stop en route. Every time, he led the field home, easily out-pacing those who thought of themselves as serious cyclists.

Arguably, Tony's ability to see both the local and the wider issues made him different politically. He was fiercely committed to his local cause, but he could always see the connections with the bigger picture. As he matured into his role over the years, he became more confident and ready to engage with wider national concerns. But he was also selective and discerning. He did not take on an endless stream of specific causes. He was careful to focus his attention only on certain issues at a time, both to avoid losing connection with his base and to allow himself to be well informed on the issues he selected. The pragmatist in him meant he would not be profligate in the use of his time on wider issues. And he was also careful to skirt issues that might alienate key elements in his political base. To the discomfort of many of his activists, he was relatively coy in his support of the divorce campaigns in 1986 and 1995. As these activists saw it, he was afraid of frightening off 'the little old ladies praying in the local churches' – little old ladies who were among his loyal voters. On abortion, too, Seanie Lambe remembers his response to those who tried to stir controversy for him on the issue: 'This is not an issue for my constituents.' He meant this in a number of senses: they had enough on their plate coping with poverty; they did not come – ever – to his clinic raising this issue in any way; the community had a long tradition of dealing collectively with unplanned pregnancy by arranging for the new baby to be cared for in the extended family.

'Who'll speak up for us now?' was the response of the women street traders whom Tony had represented on so many occasions when they heard Tony was terminally ill. Their cause ticked so many boxes for Tony. As far as he was concerned the city had taken away the community and housing of many people in the inner city when the authorities demolished the old tenement areas. Here was another attempt, as he saw it, to do down inner-city residents. This time it was taking away their livelihood, a livelihood with a long tradition. The iconic Dublin song 'Molly Malone', known the world over, was, after all, based on the story of a Dublin street trader – a fishmonger. And it was the women who were to be most affected, since most of the traders were women. Fighting the cause of powerless women who were opposed by powerful interests had an irresistible appeal for Tony; he relished the challenge and was a consistent advocate for these women.

Tony was steadfast in pursuit of his priority issues. But to be elected each time, he needed to draw support from across the constituency, not just from the core of the inner city. In every election, the tallies would tell a reassuring story. (During an election boxes full of votes come back from the polling stations, every box is opened in turn and ballot papers are emptied onto a table. These votes are carefully unfolded and placed face-up in neat piles, in preparation for the actual count. Observing this process systematically can yield 'tallies' which allow the political parties to get pretty accurate esti-mates of voting patterns at quite a local level, almost street by street.) The tallies told the Gregory camp that every box opened delivered its share of Tony votes – number ones, and crucially in the proportional representation system, number twos and later preferences. It caused endless intrigue to the Gregory team how often they saw the pattern of 'Ahern 1, Gregory 2' on voting papers, not a pattern of voting that you would have bet your house on. Undoubtedly, voters outside the inner-city core area had many diverse motives for voting for Tony: for his standing up to the political establish-ment, for serving as a voice for the poor, for his stand on animal welfare, for being an Irish language supporter, for his republican roots, and more. Each niche might bring its own share of first or later preferences. The business of winning enough electoral support outside the core base of the inner city was difficult enough, but it was made even more challenging by the regular re-shaping of the boundaries of the constituency, such as adding and then subtracting Ballyfermot. While the shaping of constituency boundaries is meant to be a fully independent process, in darker and more paranoid moments Tony might have had cause to wonder, especially since constituen-cies typically never otherwise crossed the Liffey. Yet, he survived all the slings and arrows of boundary changes.

Tony's political base in the same modest house – the family home his parents had bought and where he lived for most of his life, and where Noel continues to live – brought many advantages. It was familiar territory. It gave him serious 'street-cred' in the type of community where public representatives were more remote socially and physically; typically living a car ride away in some more salubrious surroundings. Living locally or being strongly connected locally also gave him tremendous moral authority which he used in his attacks on the drug dealers. But this was also a high-risk strategy. A high profile locally meant also being extra-vulnerable to revenge by those he annoyed. He had a status which gave him some protection, but that was no guarantee, as Veronica Guerin's family was to discover. It took personal courage to take the stands that Tony took on the drugs issue, a personal courage that is a rare find in public life in Ireland, or anywhere else come to that.

CHAPTER 9

• • • • • •

Messenger of the People

Tony and his associates took the idea of his being a messenger of the people seriously. During the crafting of the Gregory Deal, they consulted widely with local people and with those who had relevant specialist knowledge. In Pauline Kane's words, they 'showed respect' to the views of local people, for whom such consultation was a complete novelty. No one had ever asked their views before or treated them as experts on their own situation. Pauline worked for NCCCAP from early on and found the energy and enthusiasm in the Gregory camp quite intoxicating. She suddenly became 'politicised' and the discussions and action to which she was party awakened the sense of justice that had lain dormant within her. She recalls how in the early days, the group members were not shy about direct action. A public body proving resistant to their arguments in the morning (after many attempts) might find itself the site of an occupation by disaffected residents in the afternoon. The message was getting out – the people of the inner city were no longer subdued and they were not going away.

Tony's electoral success was not just a gain for Tony, it had a huge impact on local self-belief, as recalled by a local community activist:

> Tony's election symbolised people's belief that the NCCC really represented their interests. People made their own of major issues. They were operating at a completely different level. It gave us all an insight into politics. Things like the alternative (housing) plan were the topic of conversation. People got into the election count and knew what was going on. I had to learn how to explain to people about the ballot paper and the significance of how they voted. People got their first experience of

winning something – of their own power – through the NCCC.[1]

The general election in 2007 turned out to be Tony's last electoral outing. In the four-seater Dublin Central constituency, Bertie Ahern, then still Taoiseach, received a staggering 12,734 first preferences. Tony got the next highest number of first preference votes – a much more modest 4,649. Ahern was elected on the first count, Tony on the sixth, and Joe Costello (Labour) and Cyprian Brady, Bertie's Fianna Fáil running mate, on the final count. Election results can be cruel in their clarity. The voters' judgement is final, and in Tony's case not overly generous on that occasion given his long years of dedicated service to his constituency. Many of the other candidates were relative 'blow-ins' politically, or at least first-timers as Dáil candidates, such as Cyprian Brady, Pascal O'Donohue, who had been elected to Dublin City Council for Fine Gael in 2004, or Sinn Féin's Mary Lou McDonald, who had stood unsuccessfully in Dublin West in 2002 and had been elected as an MEP for Dublin in 2004. It must have given Tony pause for thought to see this pattern of results, especially to see the blow-in Cyprian Brady elected to a seat on the back of a tiny number of first preferences thanks to the monumental number of transfers he gained from Ahern – Brady's election debased the currency in terms of the effort Tony had invested to gain and retain the seat he had held for twenty-five years.

Yet, even after this disappointment, Tony's appetite for national politics seemed undiminished. A seat won was a seat won. That the independence, vigour and sweep of his approach still remained is well illustrated in this speech he made on the debate about the election of the next Taoiseach when the Dáil first met after the general election in June 2007. Here was no parish pump politician.

> On the nomination of Taoiseach, there has been some speculation in recent weeks in the media regarding why I was not involved in talks with one of the nominees, Deputy Bertie Ahern. Perhaps that was because we both

shared the same constituency and the Deputy was conscious of the priority issues on which I contested the recent election. Those issues include the need to end the two-tier health service and the scandal of the exploitation of public hospitals for private profit; the need to control the price of building land, much of which is held by a cartel of billionaire developers who have driven house prices beyond affordability for most people; the need to radically address the inequality in education, which sees less than 5% of children in some communities in Dublin Central going to third-level education; the need to strive for a fairer and more equal society; the need to safeguard our neutrality and sovereignty by ending the shameful use of Shannon Airport by United States military forces on their way to their murderous and illegal war in Iraq; the need to develop our natural resources to benefit our people and not at the behest of multinational oil companies; and the need to ensure that when a person dies in Garda custody or dies of injuries sustained while in custody, an immediate and independent investigation is conducted. These were some of the political issues on which I stood for election in Dublin Central and it is they and no other consideration whatever which will dictate the manner in which I will vote on the nomination for Taoiseach.[2]

During this last election, some of his team noticed that Tony looked thinner than usual, but had put it down to the hard physical exertions of the election, long hours pounding the pavements and climbing lampposts. He typically lost weight during the course of an election and gradually regained it when things calmed down after the election. But this time it was different. The weight did not go back on. He was very private about his illness, although gradually the evidence was there for all to see. One of the first to know the score was his political secretary.

Valerie Smith worked as Tony's secretary in the Dáil for his last eight years as a TD. She had prior experience in the Dáil, but with Fine Gael, which was hardly textbook training for work with Tony. But, as it turned out, they got on extremely well. And Valerie did actually have connections that were very relevant to her role. She had grown up in Donnycarney on

Dublin's northside – Charlie Haughey country – and had gone to school in St Columba's national school on the North Strand, a school that Tony had later spoken up for in the Dáil. Each day after school, Valerie would go to her aunt's shop in Summerhill to be minded and she would serve behind the counter to pass the time until her mother collected her after work. (Her aunt's surname was Morris, but the aunt had become known locally as Mrs Morrissey because the locals felt that the name had a better ring to it with that embellishment!) As it happens, Tony himself was a regular customer – another from the 'Dublin is a village' collection.

During 2007, Valerie had been on extended sick leave, and close to the time she was due back she got a call from Tony wondering if she could come back a little early as he now had his own health difficulties. Having been off for a while, she hadn't actually seen Tony in some time. She recalls how he always used to give a little cough as he came down the corridor to alert her to his arrival. On this occasion, however, he called out as he approached: 'Val, I'm coming around the corner and I don't want you to get a fright.' Val was shocked at what she saw: 'He looked so fragile, drawn, and that awful grey look was in his face.' There followed more than a year as he battled with the illness. But the show went on. He came in every day through his illness, barring days he had to have treatment or when he was hospitalised. Even then, he was in regular contact by phone each day. And he remained an intense competitor in the political game right to the end.

Tony, like every politician, knew how vital media coverage was. A story in the newspapers, on television or the radio that featured Tony was a way of keeping his name in voters' minds. There was the additional advantage in the fiercely competitive worlds of constituency electoral politics that if Tony was mentioned in a story, it reduced the chances of the journalist seeking or being given the space for the views of a competing TD or candidate from the constituency. Over time he developed a rapport with various journalists who might contact him for a comment or for some 'inside track' on how he saw a story unfolding. One such journalist was RTÉ crime correspondent Paul Reynolds. Drugs and crime issues in Tony's constituency provided the two with frequent opportunities to liaise. Inevitably, in the later stages of his illness, Tony was out of the picture to some degree. On one occasion in the months close to the end, there was a murder in East Wall and Joe Costello, Tony's local rival TD, was interviewed on RTÉ. Tony was on the phone like a flash to Paul to remonstrate at not being contacted – 'I'm not dead yet' was his rebuke. 'I knew you were sick and didn't want to disturb you,' was Paul's very reasonable reply. Even in the advanced stages of his terminal illness, the competitive political instincts and urge for publicity were undimmed.[3]

Gradually the word about his illness filtered out among Tony's friends and connections, but he dealt with it all very privately. As happens in many friendships, long passages of time might elapse before Liz Doyle and Tony would see each other. Whenever they did meet, Liz would get the same stock response from Tony as everyone else: when she asked him how he was, he would invariably grunt 'Terrible' in mock misery and self-depre-cation. She recalled the first time meeting Tony after news of his serious illness had emerged. They met up to go to a funeral together. She asked him, 'How are you?' in a more meaningful way than usual. He responded, 'What do you think?'

In his final months, Tony registered a victory over Independent News-papers. They had angered him over their coverage of details of his illness, and the manner in which they had 'door-stepped' his brother, Noel, in rela-tion to it. Tony regarded this as an invasion of his privacy and had made a formal complaint to the newly established Press Ombudsman, who found in his favour.[4] Independent Newspapers appealed against the judgement and this appeal was subsequently heard by the Press Council, who again found against the newspaper. (Despite this incident, the newspaper company still found it in its heart – or its commercial interest – to publish a twelve-page special supplement in the *Evening Herald* on day of his funeral.)

While Tony remained true to his principles throughout his career, a certain mellowness may have crept in in later years. Although candid that he would vote against Brian Cowen's election as Taoiseach, Tony still made a point of making generous comments in the Dáil about Cowen just before his election, partly undoubtedly because of their shared roots in Offaly, his mother's home county. Tony had also had dealings with Cowen as Minister for Foreign Affairs and had grown to respect his approach. Maureen O'Sullivan recalls that he was quite ill at that point with the cancer that ultimately killed him, but that he had been very determined to be present for this short speech. Tony actually re-arranged the times of his chemotherapy treatment regime on the day so as to be present in the Dáil for Brian Cowen's election. In his few words of good wishes to Cowen, Tony managed also to make some political points, starting off, in his beloved Irish, by praising the Taoiseach designate's approach to the Irish language. The extract also includes a collector's item: a word of gratitude from Tony to Bertie Ahern, a fellow constituency TD and therefore a longterm rival.

> **Os rud é nach mbeidh an deis agam labhairt anseo níos déanaí i ndiaidh an toghcháin don Taoiseach agus os rud é go bhfuil sé soiléir go mbeidh tromlach sa Dáil ag an dTeachta Brian Cowen agus go mbeidh sé ina Thaoiseach i gceann tamaill gearr, ba mhaith liomsa an deis a ghlacadh comhghairdeas a dhéanamh leis, go háirithe de bharr an seasamh láidir a ghlac sé ar son na Gaeilge, ár dteanga náisiúnta, nuair a toghadh é ina uachtarán ar Fhianna Fáil.**

> **Since I won't be able to be here later after the election of the Taoiseach and since it is clear that Deputy Cowen will have a majority and that he will soon be Taoiseach, I would like to take the opportunity to congratulate him, especially because of his strong stand on Irish, our national language, when he was elected President of Fianna Fáil.**

> **As my late mother was born and reared in County Offaly and as I spent my childhood holidays on a small farm on the edge of the Bog of Allen,**

in the shadow of Croghan Hill—

Deputy Ruairí Quinn: Now we know.

A deputy: It did the Deputy no harm.

Deputy Tony Gregory: I welcome the fact that County Offaly will shortly have the great honour, for the first time, of being the home county of a Taoiseach. Of course, this does not mean that I intend voting for Deputy Cowen.

Deputy Bernard J. Durkan: The Deputy is breaking my heart.

Deputy Tony Gregory: However, on this occasion I want to say that Deputy Cowen has my good wishes. This is a great occasion for him, his family and his county.

I hope that in his term as Taoiseach, Deputy Cowen will see the justice in taking steps to end the divisive inequalities that exist in Ireland today, particularly in our health service, in education and in housing. It is my view that the increasing social inequality of recent years is the major issue facing all of us elected by the people to this house.

I would like to take this opportunity to record my thanks to my constituency colleague, Deputy Bertie Ahern, for his recent kind words regarding my health and to wish him well. Go raibh maith agat, a Cheann Comhairle.[5]

Tony's spirit fought on to the end. David Norris recalls interviewing him late in his illness for a programme on Newstalk radio. Tony was clearly in very poor shape physically, but was also determined to proceed with the interview. Once the interview got under way, Norris recalls Tony being transformed. His spirit came shining through. He engaged in thoughtful and reflective conversation, summoning up various memories from his childhood and beyond.

Valerie Smith decided to pay Tony a visit on what was to be his last birthday while he was a patient in hospital. As it happened, he didn't feel up to actual visitors, so she left her gift and a musical birthday card for him at reception. She later cringed as she recalled the title of the song in the musical card – the only one the shop had – 'you have all the time in the world'. Sadly, this was not to prove an apt message. Weeks later, Valerie was to get a call to say that Tony had passed away on 2 January 2009. Days before his death, Tony had managed to text Valerie, wishing her and her family the best for Christmas. For her, that symbolised the way he had kept going right to the end.

Those invited had paid their respects to Tony as he lay in the coffin in the front room in the house where he grew up. The time came to close the coffin. A huge crowd of those close to his cause had assembled outside. Noel was carefully allocating positions of responsibility and ranking in the cortege as the coffin, draped in the Starry Plough – the flag of the Irish republican Left – was held by those charged with carrying it the short journey along the thronged cul-de-sac over the Royal Canal and left down the bank of the canal on the other side before a right turn and then into the grounds of St Agatha's church where a huge crowd had gathered. The cortege made its way with dignity along the route, led by a lone piper. Those carrying the coffin concentrated hard, anxious not to slip in the icy conditions underfoot. Making their way down the canal path to the church was tricky, but there was a determination to follow this route out of respect for Noel's wishes. It was a bright, sunny morning for the funeral mass the next day. A roll call of key figures in politics, public administration and civil society turned up to join the huge numbers of locals. As the coffin emerged from the church on its final journey, a ripple of applause broke out among those who had lined the roadway to bid their last farewell. It was clear that someone of importance was being saluted on their final journey. One sign was the huge effort the Garda Síochána had put into supporting the funeral. As Johnny Connolly noted, it was as if the force wished to declare its thanks to a friend – a critical friend certainly, but ultimately a friend in the fight against crime and drugs in the inner city.[6] Maureen O'Sullivan made it clear that the graveyard was for the people who had been longtime supporters, it was not to be a photo-opportunity for anyone jumping on the bandwagon. It was a grumpy note that jarred even with some of his own supporters. But it was true to Tony. At times, he did grumpy.

Tony's death was a big story. It was clear that the people of Dublin felt they had lost one of their own. Strangers asked each other had they heard the news. Many tributes were paid informally. Among the formal ones there were two that Tony might have valued especially – from Brian Cowen as Taoiseach and from the City Council.

FROM BRIAN COWEN:

As Taoiseach, Brian Cowen paid a generous and apt tribute in his speech in the Dáil after Tony's death as is evident in the following extract:

> Connolly's Irish Citizen Army had championed the cause of Dublin's working class during the 1913 Lock Out. At Tony's funeral, the blue and white of the Starry Plough flag, the same flag that is synonymous with the Citizen Army, draped Tony Gregory's coffin on his final journey to Balgriffin Cemetery. As the people who attended his funeral applauded as the funeral hearse brought him on his last journey, I watched and felt there was something very moving and deeply appropriate about that scene. The Irish Citizen Army served neither King nor Kaiser but Ireland and her people. So too did Tony Gregory. The people knew it and appreciated it greatly. He was a hardworking Teachta Dála – a true messenger of the people – who served his community with sincerity, commitment and skill.[7]

FROM THE CITY COUNCIL:

At a meeting days after Tony's death, the Lord Mayor, city councillors and the City Manager paid generous tribute to him, as recorded in this extract from the minutes of the meeting.

The Lord Mayor opened the meeting with a silent prayer followed by a minute's silence as a mark of respect to the late Tony Gregory TD and former member of Dublin City Council. She paid tribute to Tony, saying he had been a loyal servant of Dublin who fought tirelessly for his constituents and had a total grasp of the issues affecting the inner city. She said his contribution to the city had been enormous. Members of the City Council who also spoke in praise of his contribution to the political life of Dublin's inner city, and the city as a whole, and indeed the island of Ireland included Councillors M. O'Sullivan, C. Burke, R. McGinley, Eric Byrne, E. Costello, J. Collins, T. Stafford, M. O'Shea, J. Carmichael, M. Fitzpatrick, B. Tormey, S. Kenny and M. Frehill. His dedication to his constituents, his tireless work on their behalf, his generosity with his time, with his expertise, political knowledge and acumen were highlighted by many. He was fearless in confronting drug barons operating in his area and was responsible for highlighting the drugs problem in the inner city long before drug abuse emerged as a more widespread issue. It was agreed that his untimely death was a great loss to the city, to his constituents, and especially to his family, friends and close associates. The City Manager, on his own behalf and on behalf of the staff, joined with the members in expressing condolences to Tony's family and friends and fully concurred with all the tributes that had been paid to him.[8]

The media were also effusive in their attention and favourable comment. Déaglán de Breadún, the *Irish Times* political correspondent, reflected on Tony's death, and very aptly focused in part on the 'Bertie issue':

A quiet, dogged individual, Gregory had plenty of personal charm but no aspirations to be a leader in his own right.

I shall miss our lunchtime conversations in the Leinster House canteen and his mordant observations on his constituency rival, former Taoiseach Bertie Ahern. Gregory was irritated by the wave of tribunal-induced sympathy for his competitor that he encountered on the doorsteps in the last general election. He recounted with some annoyance how he was being told, 'We have to vote for poor Bertie, he's in trouble.' He would have smiled wryly at the sympathy expressed on his demise by the former Fianna Fáil leader.[9]

Reflecting on Tony's long and effective contribution to the Dail at the time of his death, the editorial writer of *The Irish Times* observed that 'Parliament is diminished by his absence.'[10]

The boy from Ballybough had done his parents' memory and his community proud. He had won a precious scholarship to secondary school; he had been an honoured teacher; he had had an exceptional career as a local and national politician; he had negotiated with Charles Haughey (and Garret FitzGerald) for his vote to elect a government; he had delivered a historic package of reforms for his local area; he had competed in elections with Bertie Ahern, for long the most powerful electoral force in the land; he had walked out on Ronald Reagan; he had shaken hands with Fidel Castro; he had been the public conscience on the issue of drugs; he had gone to prison in support of the street traders; he had constantly sought reforms in many areas, from crime to animal welfare. Most of all, he had put Dublin's north inner city on the national map politically and he had helped to restore to its people their voice and confidence. He had won the respect of friend and foe, and a special place in the heart of his native city.

APPENDIX 1

• • • • • • •

The Gregory Deal

Note: this document was typed in pre-computer days with several pages left blank for possible later additions - in many cases not needed. Hence the unusual pagination of the document.

AGREEMENTS REACHED BY

CHARLIE HAUGHEY T.D. AND TONY GREGORY T.D.

———————————————

-1-

In our discussions we put forward the same list of issues to each leader. We now indicate the response of Fianna Fail to these issues.

1. EMPLOYMENT.

(A) Environmental Public Works Scheme.

1. Mr. Haughey committed himself to providing a budget of £4,000,000 for 1982 to employ 500 men.

2. The scheme will be made permanent and adequate finance made available to ensure that it fully absorbs the maximum number of people who can be usefully engaged on environmental work for the benefit of local communities.

(B) 27 Acres Port and Docks Site.

PORT AND DOCKS SITE

1. Site to be acquired by legislation before 30th June 1982. Legislation to appoint three Commissioners, one of whom is to be selected by the Chairman of the Inner City Authority. These Commissioners will be the planning authority for the site and will be responsible for the development of the site.

-2-

2. The Inner City Authority will select the consultant
    architects to be appointed and approve the development plan.

3. The development plan will follow broadly the following
    allocation of site use.

    6 acres for office accommodation.
    10 acres local authority housing.
    8 acres for industrial development.
    3 acres for leisure and recreational purposes including
    a multi-purpose leisure centre.

Port and Docks Site.

This will be acquired by legislation and developed by three
Commissioners appointed in the legislation on behalf of the state.
A project team of architects, planners, industrial, financial and
administrative experts will be set up to accelerate this development
and to bring on stream the residential and the industrial and
commercial job making phases as soon as possible. Our general
Inner City employment programme assumes that some of the 400,000
square feet will be ready in 1983/84.

A map showing Fianna Fail's proposals for the Port and Dock site,
3 acres of which will be set aside for a leisure and sports complex,
is attached.

One commissioner to be appointed by I.C.A.
Architects to be appointed/selected by I.C.A.

-3-

Sports and Recreational Facilities.

A multi-purpose leisure complex will be provided on the Port
and Docks site on the lines of that built by Tolka Rovers. 3
acres will be reserved on the P & D site for this complex and
£½m. provided under the Department of Education scheme.

C. The export of raw materials.

(i)   The national Enterprise Agency will have extended powers
        and will take on specific responsibility for the development
        of our natural resources.

(ii)   As a demonstration of the Governments committment
        Clondalkin Paper Mills will be nationalised if there is
        no other immediate option within three months.

D. Inner City Employment Programme.

(i)   Mr. Haughey gave a committment that in the period 1982 -
        1985 3,746 new jobs would be created in the Inner City.

(ii)   The I.D.A. grant for attracting new industries will be
        increased from 45% to 60%.

(iii)   That the I.D.A. set a job creation target of 1,000 jobs.

-5-

E. Corporation Maintenance Workforce.

The Fianna Fail budget to Dublin Corporation will enable
the employment of an additional 150 craftsmen to provide
a more acceptable maintenance service.

F. Major investment in the construction industry.

(1) Mr. Haughey committed himself to t he maximum housing
    capital projections within the capacity of Dublin Corporation.
    This involves an increase from 1,350 new houses in 1982
    to 2000 in 1984.

(2) He further agreed to provide additional finance to build
    1600 houses in 1982 with a budget of £91,000,000 should
    Dublin Corporation be capable of meeting that target.

(3) Within that programme a guarantee was given on the immediate
    commencement in 1982 of work on 440 new houses in the North
    Inner City Area.

(4) A further guarantee that work would commence in 1983 on an
    additional 197 houses in the North Centre City Area.

(5) Mr. Haughey agreed to separate budget allocation for Inner
    City Housing with (2) above.

(6) Maintenance of Corporation dwellings will be brought to a
    more acceptable standard by the elimination of a cut back
    introduced by the Coalition by restoration to the maintenance

-6-

budget of 40% of the proceeds of housing sales.   This
will be over and above the £16,000,000 allocation.

(7)   Additional funds will be available from an increased
      budgetry allocation of £20,000,000 to the Corporation
      from Central funds.

DUBLIN CORPORATION HOUSING PROGRAMME

The Dublin Corporation have confirmed the following
housing capital projections:

	No. of Houses.	£ million.
1982	1350	76.87
1983	1750	87.5
1984	2000	100.00

We confirm that these amounts of capital monies at least will
be made available to the Corporation.   It was also agreed
that £91,000,000 will be made available to Dublin Corporation
this year to increase the construction target to 1600
houses.   The long term committment as outlined above to provide
2000 houses in 1984 is a major advance and should greatly
relieve the housing emergency in Dublin.   The committment to
Inner City housing outlined below is perhaps the most
significant development so far in inner city renewal.

-7-

Northern Inner City Housing.

Attached is a Dublin Corporation list of sites available for the
provision of inner-city housing.

Despite the reduced output by Dublin Corporation this year,
Fianna Fail are prepared on the basis of the attached list of
sites to guarantee the commencement immediately in 1982 of work
on 440 units in the Northern Inner City area.

This figure of 440 is arrived at as follows:

Designated Areas: Sections A,B,C,D.   213

List 2

Seville Place/Oriel Street I	33
Mountjoy Street	31
Portland Row/Empress Place	24
Glasnevin	80

List 3

Rutland Street	60	<u>228</u>
		441

-8-

We also guarantee that all necessary preliminaries will be expedited so that building may commence on the following sections early in 1983:

Russell Street   33
Phibsboro Road   100
Seville Place   64

Acquisition of land for housing.

An immediate special fund will be provided to Dublin Corporation to acquire land for long term housing purposes.

C.P.O. on Upper Oriel Street.

The Development Plan for the Sheriff Street area to include a C.P.O. order on Upper Oriel Street.

-9-

DUBLIN CORPORATION CURRENT BUDGETARY ALLOCATION

WE CONFIRM THAT AN ADDITIONAL £20 MILLION WILL BE MADE
AVAILABLE FROM CENTRAL FUNDS TO ENABLE DUBLIN CORPORATION
TO MAINTAIN SERVICES AT ACCEPTABLE LEVEL.

-10-

MAINTENANCE

Dublin Corporation's budget for maintenance of houses and flats, which amounted to £7½m in 1981, has been cut by £2.7m this year, as the result of a Government decision to take all the proceeds from the sale of Corporation houses, instead of leaving 40% of the proceeds with the Corporation for maintenance. Fianna Fail will restore this 40%. Under Fianna Fail the total budget for maintenance in 1982 will be approximately £10m. per annum thus enabling up to 150 extra maintenance men to be taken on.

Modernisation of Substandard Dwellings programme.

Fianna Fail will commence in 1982 a programme to fit all Corporation flats that lack bathroom or shower facilities with showers. Work will begin on the 183 flats at Liberty House in 1982, and it will be possible to fit almost 500 flats per annum. It is estimated that almost 3000 flats in all are without such facilities. £1,000,000 additional allocation will be made available for this purpose

-11-

(8)   That Central Government will provide the necessary
funds to acquire immediately the 4 acre-site at
Shandon Park.

The development plan for the Sheriff Street are to
include a C.P.O. order on Upper Oriel Street.

An immediate special fund be provided to Dublin
Corporation to acquire land for long-term housing
purposes.

A £1m revolving fund be allocated to Dublin, this
will be used to acquisition and rehabilitation of
residential property.

TRAINING.

Acceptance of new industries in the centre-city to be based
on prior agreement with AnCO re. training of Inner City
Workforce.

That a specific objective be to re-train 300-500 adult
inner city dwellers along with the main objective of training
and placing 300-500 young inner city dwellers in employment
per annum.

-12-

TAX.

5% Tax on derelict sites increasing by 1% per annum.

That the Corporation be empowered to develop intensive uses
of amenity value on derelict land.

That a special tax on existing and future office development
based on 2% of rent income (estimated) to produce an income
of £1,000,000, the resulting finance to go to Inner City
Renewal.

Bank taxation to be increased progressively and a white
paper be brought out to examine how banks and financial
institutions operate and how they can be controlled and
democratised.

Capital taxation of unearned income to be increased.

Tax on Banks and Financial Institutions.

It is important that banks and financial institutions should
be seen to bear their fair share of taxation. Fianna Fail
intend to introduce a permanent form of taxation, following
receipt of the recommendations of the Commission on Taxation.

In the interim a special bank levy of £20m. will be imposed
in 1982, £5m. more than proposed in the January budget. A

-13-

1% levy on insurance company turnover will also be introduced
to bring in an extra £6m. and Corporation Tax will be brought
forward yielding £36m.

Aids to new Industries.

A tax-holding period of 3-4 years be granted to new industries.
The application of the I.D.A. grant to discriminate in favour
of labour intensive industries.

-14-

HEALTH.

1.   Free Medical Cards for all Social Welfare Pensioners
      and the scheme to be extended to all other categories
      of pensioners in need.

2.   Fianna Fail agree to expand home help services.

3.   Fianna Fail will act on findings of review body on
      travelling people.

4.   Fianna Fail agree to set up a system of regular and
      rigorous inspection of all institutions caring for
      children, disabled, mentally ill and elderly whether
      public or private.

5.   Fianna Fail agree to take steps to control costs of
      drugs for the Health Service.

6.   Fianna Fail will give a serious committment to tackle
      drug abuse and to provide proper treatment facilities.

7.   Each community care area in Dublin will have a
      monitoring committee which will adequately represent
      those using the health service.

8.   A special section of the Dept. of Health will be set
      up to cater for the needs of the disabled in the community.

-15-

9.   Existing Neighbourhood Youth Projects now being run by
       the Eastern Health Board will be funded and staffed along
       the same lines as the Limerick N.Y.P. model and will have
       a local Management Committee structure. A committment is
       given to extend these projects in 1983.

FAMILY AND CHILDREN.

Welfare.

1.   Will establish a National Council for Children, as planned
       already by Fianna Fail.

2.   Will establish regional Child Care Authorities, along
       principles set out in Task Force Report.

3.   We are prepared to set up an all party Orieachtas Committee
       on Child and Family Welfare and will seek agreement to this.

4.   Will support national arrangements for marriage guidance
       and conciliation. Will consider Bristol Scheme.

Laws.

1.   Will prepare new Children's Bill. Preparations were in
       train when Fianna Fail left office.

-16-

2.   Will raise age of criminal responsibility substantially.
      We accept 12 as minimum.

3.   Will introduce legislation to establish Family Courts
      system to servie child and family law cases.

4.   Will discuss point re. Court Act 1981 - and relegating
      family matters to District Court.

5.   On constitutional ban on divorce-will await findings of
      the Special Committee on Marriage Breakdown.

6.   Abolition of illegitimacy - will pursue the studies which
      are already in train.

7.   Adoption system - will review with a view to reform.

8.   Extension of eligibility for adoption to legitmate children
      in special circumstances. We will examine this situation.

9.   Transfer of oversight of adoption system to Department of
      Health. Yes, we are basically in favour of unified
      responsibility under Department of Health for children.

-17-

SOCIAL WELFARE.

1. General:
    We accept need for a major review of Social Welfare
    Department's are of work. There is an urgent need to
    remove anomalies in the legislation and to review the
    whole operation of the Department in relation to the
    increased size, scope and new needs. Major commission to
    review the entire operation will be set up.

2. Overhaul of Supplementary Welfare System:
    Fianna Fail agree on the need for a general overhaul
    to include the following measures;
    -   better training of all staff.
    -   better publicity.
    -   more generous rates.
    -   independent appeals system.
    -   independent appeals system for all Social Welfare.
    -   Autumn increase in rates to compensate for additional
        inflation.
    -   Double weeks in September and Xmas. (School books,
        Clothes, Xmas expenses)
    -   Other minor act reforms.

3. Review of Social Welfare consolidated act 1980 section
    regarding Social Welfare benefits in areas of Employer/
    Workers disputes.

-18-

COMMUNITY DEVELOPMENT.

Setting up of a National Community Development agency which would directly fund local community organisations and other groups working for or with the disadvantaged.

This agency would have the same financial resources as Combat Poverty i.e. £2,000,000.

This new agency will have Statutory powers.

Existing community projects (e.g. North Centre City Community Action Project, The Combat Poverty Projects in Cork and Waterford) will be funded at a level comparable with the original contracted-out projects.

The Chairman of the Inner City Authority will appoint one person to the National Committee.

EDUCATION.

It is our intention to declare the Dublin North Inner City an Educational Priority Area. This will enable positive discrimination to be exercised in favour of a socially deprived area, and special measures taken by suspending normal Department of Education rules.

-19-

Primary Education.

From this decision to declare the North Inner City an Educational Priority Area Fianna Fail will provide the primary schools in the North Inner City with:

- An improved pupil-teacher ratio, of the order of 1 teacher to every 25 pupils.
- Increased number of Remedial Teachers on the basis of one per National School or per 200 pupils, whichever is the lesser, and improved remedial facilities.
- An improved psycholoical service. At least 2 or 3 full-time Psychologists would be required to liaise with the Remedial Teachers in the primary schools.
- In addition Educational Family Liaison Officers will be appointed, to improve liaison between the families of the individual pupil and his school so that educational motivation can be improved. At present there is a problem of lack of contact between the families and the schools, resulting in a lack of motivation in the pupils. The appointment of Educational Family Liaison Officers is designed to effect a major improvement in this situation.
- Certain clearly beneficial results of the Rutland Street project can and will now be applied. Schools would be allowed to develop individualised programmes on an ad hoc basis, to be evaluated and modified as

-20-

necessary by Inspectors of the Department of Education. Irish
for example might be taught more in the context of an Irish
studies programme in this area.

Secondary Education.

Secondary education is relatively little availed of by Inner
City families. This is partly because Inner City families, by
reason of their exceptionally low and uncertain incomes, are
compelled to forego education for their children because these
children must become wage earners as early as possible, normally
in dead-end casual occupations. There is also a tradition inherited
from before the days of free secondary education, when a small
fee was charged by the voluntary schools, of non-participation
in secondary education.

The basic problem with the existing Inner City schools such
as O'Connell School is not lack of places but the lack of a
full range of facilities. As a result second-level schools
in the area have attracted children mainly from outside the
City area and a number of these schools have now either been
closed altogether, or have been relocated (Eccles Street, North
Great Georges Street, Dominick Street, and the Sisters of Charity
School in Gardiner Street.) The schools, if they obtained the
necessary extra facilities, could concentrate on serving the
Northern Inner City population rather than a wider catchment area.
What is required therefore, and what Fianna Fail will provide

the following:

- An improvement pupil/teacher ratio, the aim being an
  average of 1 teacher to 14 pupils. This will be related
  however to the percentage of Inner City pupils taken
  in.

- An increased range of facilities including provision
  of woodwork, metalwork, building construction, typing,
  home economics.

- The provisions of pre-employment courses (see below
  under From School to Work)

- Incceased Remedial Teachers (1 per 100 pupils)

- and improved psychological service to liaise with the
  Career Guidance, Remedial and Educational Family Liaison
  Officers.

- A Community School entering for 3-400$ pupils with
  the increased facilities.

- Provision to encourage the secondary schools to undertake
  as part of their Physical Education Programme physical
  activity of an 'outward bound' type, as it is called
  in other   countries.

Special Family-Income Education Support.

We will provide, where necessary, Special Family-Income
Educational Support in these exceptionally deprived areas, so
that children can continue whole time education up to and
including third-level, both university and technological. This
family income educational support scheme will consist of a special

-22-

annual supplement in addition to the grants now available
under the Higher Education Grant Scheme on an income limit
basis.

In this way we intend to break the vicious cycle of lack of
educational and vocational attainment which is a major
impediment to raising the social and economic opportunities
and the quality of life enjoyed by the people of the Inner City.

In addition to the Family-Income Educational Support Scheme,
a number of other specific educational measures will be
undertaken including the following:

-     Special adult education schemes to raise the education
      level of adults, thus raising the levels of their
      employment opportunities.
-     A special pre-school facility will be provided as a
      special type of pilot scheme for children of Inner
      City areas.

From School to Work.

In addition, it is vital to provide pre-employment courses, not
ordinarily available to the voluntary schools, linked to AnCO
and to job prospects. These are related to our proposals that
AnCO should substantially increase its intake from the Inner
City and give priority to this area.   The objective will be to
reverse the spiral of deprivation, ensuring that trained people
from the Inner City obtain trades. Vandalism and lack of
motivation at present spring principally from the poor job
prospects of Inner City dwellers.

-23-

SPECIFIC COMMITTMENTS.

<u>Seville Place School</u>: We accept that Seville Place represents
an exceptional situation and that A special effort will be made
both at pre-school and primary level. Resources will be provided
for a pilot pre-school, and the primary school will be re-organised
along the lines of the Rutland Street Scheme with special
provision made for slow learners.

<u>Community School</u>: A 300/400 pupil second level community school
to be provided on the office of public works site at Lower
Gardiner Street, adjacent to Department of Education premises.

Estimated cost £3 million.

<u>Youth Encounter Project</u>: Based on the experience of the Youth
Encounter Project in Rutland Strret that Y.E.P.'s be set up in;

1. Sheriff Street/North Wall.
2. William Street/Ballybough.
3. East Wall.

<u>School Scheme</u>: It was agreed that within the Educational
Priority Area all school books be provided free for locally
oriented schools.

<u>Rutland Street Primary School</u>: The continuing process of
educational development proposed by the management of the
Rutland Street Primary School be immediately agreed to by
the Dept. of Education.

-24-

INNER CITY DEVELOPMENT AUTHORITY.

GENERAL.

The New Inner City Development Authority which will take over the duties and functions of the existing interdepartmental Committee will operate on the same lines as SFADCO in Shannon.

AUTHORITY AND FUND.

It will have its own special fund with delegated authority in specific areas to enable it to achieve its objectives. It will report to the new Minister of State in the Department of the Environment. The new Authority will have its own budget and grant making capacity up to an agreed amount.

It is envisaged that the budget for 1982 will be at least £2m.

The new Authority will carry on, develop and expand the functions of the existing Inter-Departmental Co-ordinating Committee and will be allocated additional functions and responsibilities as seem necessary from time to time.

-25-

MEMBERSHIP.

The Committee will consist of a Chairman who will have a
general public affairs/business background with representatives
from the Departments of Industry and Energy, Labour, Finance
and Environment, the Dublin Corporation, the I.D.A., ICC,
AnCO, the National Board of Science and Technology and 2 or
3 persons with a special knowledge of the socio-economic
circumstances prevailing the inner city.

SECRETARIAT.

A full time adequate Secretariat, headed up by a Chief
Executive, will br provided for authority.

CHAIRMAN.

Chairman of new inner-city Authority to be nominated by Tony
Gregory and to have power to nominate 5 members.

-26-

LEAD IN PETROL.

There are EEC directives requiring stringent controls on lead
levels in petrol. Fianna Fail accept the necessity to comply
with these directives as soon as possible. The issue is closely
connected with the continued operation of the Whitegate Oil
Refinery. It is an essential part of Fianna Fail's overall
energy policy that Ireland have a major oil refinery capacity
of her own. Our objective is a new modern oil refinery with
the full range of down-stream industries provided in agreement
with a major oil producer and in a position ultimately to
refine our own indigenous supplies.   Such a refinery would of
course meet the most stringent specifications. In the meantime
the investment required to update Whitegate will be investigated
in the context of the State's future plans for a major oil
refinery.

LOCAL AUTHORITY BY RENTS.

The rent increase on all substandard dwellings will be withdrawn immediately.

LOCAL AUTHORITY S.D.A. LOANS.

Interest rates will be reduced from 15½% to 12½% and fixed at the time of the signing of the contract.

DEVELOPMENT LAND CAPITAL GAINS TAX.

Capital gains at 40% will be levied on profits accruing to sales of land and buildings. A higher tax at 45% will be applied where planning permission has been granted for change from a lower to a higher value use (e.g. from argriculture to residential or industry to offices)

JUSTICE.

That the Curragh Military Detnetion Centre be closed before the end of this year.

TRANSPORT.

1. That the Eastern by-pass Inner City relief route will not be proceeded with and that the incoming Minister for the Environment will instruct Dublin City Council not to proceed in any-way on that project.
2. All available resources to be applied to the implementation of C.I.E.'s rapid rail scheme.
3. The Dublin Transport Authority will actively discourage the use of the private motor-car within city centre limits and will pursue as far as possible a policy of pedestrianisation within the said area.

-30-

With regard to all of the proposals contained above unless otherwise stated steps shall be taken to initiate the proposals within 3 months of the formation of the Government.

Signed: Tony Gregory: *[signature]*

                           Charlie Haughey: *[signature]*

In the presence of   Michael Mullen: *[signature]*

                                          8th [?] 1982

• • • • • • •

Tony's Notes for His Last Dáil Speech

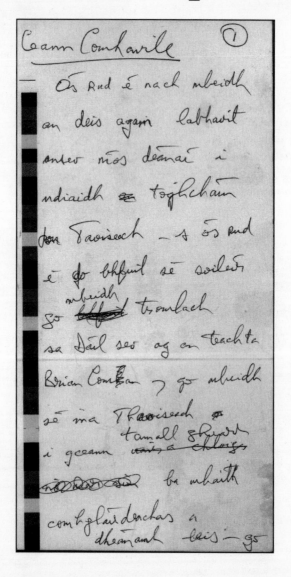

h-áirithe de-hhord an seasamh ②
láidir a ghlac sé ar
son na Gaeilge ár
teanga náisiúnta nuair
a toghadh é mar Uachtarán
ar 7.7.

— I would also like to
~~welcome the~~ say C.C.
that as my late mother was
born & reared in Co. Offaly
& as I spent my own
childhood holidays on
a small ~~~~ farm
on the edge of the Bog
of Allen near the foot
of Croghan Hill

③ I welcome the fact that
Co. Offaly will shortly have the
great honour of being
the home county for the
first time of a Taoiseach
— this does not mean
that I will be
voting for Deputy Cowen
but he certainly has
my good wishes on
what is clearly a
great occasion for him
& his family & country

225

TONY GREGORY

(4) I would hope (liked to) that in his term as T.

that he may see the [crossed out] taking steps to end justice in [crossed out] the divisive social inequalities that exist partic. in the Health [crossed out] in Education & in Housing, in Ireland today

It is my view that the increasing social inequality of recent years is the major issue forcing all of us who are elected by the people to this House.

(5) I would also like to record my thanks to Deputy [crossed out] my constituency colleague Deputy Ahern for his kind words recently regarding my health — [crossed out] spoke [crossed out] [crossed out] wish him well also.

Go raibh maith agat a C.C,

226

Footnotes

CHAPTER 1

1. *Hot Press* interview published 23 January 2009 and radio interview with David Norris.

2. Jim Sheridan, email communication, 3 January 2010.

3. From interview with Tony Gregory, 'A city playground' by Alanna Gallagher, *The Sunday Times,* 1 August 2004.

4. The incident is recorded on p71 of the book *Lockout Dublin 1913* by Pádraig Yeates (Dublin: Gill and Macmillan, 2000). Tony also referred to the incident at some length in his interview with David Norris on Newstalk radio in the latter half of 2008.

5. 'Gregory's Trek', interview with Tony Gregory by Macdara Doyle, *In Dublin,* 1992.

6. Radio interview with David Norris.

7. *Hot Press* interview published 23 January 2009.

8. Interview with Liz Doyle.

9. Radio interview with David Norris.

10. Richie Ryan TD, Dáil Debates, 20 May 1965.

11. Tony Gregory, 'Personality Profile – A Student of Life', pp2-3 in *Education – The Magazine of Ireland's Education Industry,* November/December, 1995.

12. Power, S. (2000), 'Dublin 1965-69', *Irish Geography* 33, 2, pp199-212, http://www.ucd.ie/gsi/pdf/33-2/ballymun.pdf.

13. Dáil Éireann Ceisteanna – Questions. Oral Answers. - Dublin Tenements. Thursday, 24 October 1963.

14. Declan Costello TD, Dáil Éireann Adjournment Debate. – Dublin Dangerous Buildings. Tuesday, 18 June 1963, http://debates.oireachtas.ie/dail/1963/06/18/00039.asp.

15. Richie Ryan TD, Dáil Debates, 20 May 1965.

16. 'Protest staged at dispensary', *The Irish Times,* 16 September 1965; 'Caravans given to homeless families, *The Irish Times,* 20 October 1965.

17. 'Still Flying Solo', the Rachel Borrill interview with Tony Gregory, *Ireland on Sunday*, 26 July 1998.

18. Nell McCafferty, 'Sinn Féin March to Cork Continues', *The Irish Times*, 22 December 1970.

19. 'Personality Profile – A Student of Life', pp2-3 in *Education – The Magazine of Ireland's Education Industry*, November/December 1995.

20. Ann Marie Hourihane, 'The old school ties that bind divide two Coláiste Eoin boys', *Sunday Tribune*, 26 May 2002.

21. Leslie O'Neill, 'Where teacher and pupil were equal'? *Irish Press*, 22 February 1982.

22. Ann Marie Hourihane, 'The old school ties that bind divide two Coláiste Eoin boys', *Sunday Tribune*, 26 May 2002.

23. 'Tony Gregory had to leap many barriers to his education', *The Irish Times*, 31 March 1998

CHAPTER 2

1. This information on date and number of members was credited to Tony Gregory by Brian Hanley and Scott Millar (2009), *The Lost Revolution – The Story of the Official IRA and The Workers' Party* (Dublin: Penguin Ireland) p84.

2. Accessed at http://cedarlounge.files.wordpress.com/2008/06/dhac-1969.pdf, 3 September 2011.

3. Hanley and Millar (2009) p88-9.

4. Reported in piece entitled 'MacGiolla describes direct rule as one-man dictatorship', *The Irish Times*, 3 April 1972.

5. 'Gregory says WP not democratic', *The Irish Times*, 9 June 1982.

6. Anonymous, 'Costello – A biographical and political analysis of his life and achievements', pp5-14 in *Seamus Costello 1939-1977, Irish Republican Socialist – Political Biography and Tributes from his friends and comrades* (Dublin: The Seamus Costello Memorial Committee).

7. Tony Gregory, 'Seamus – The People's Councillor', pp17–23 in *Seamus Costello 1939-1977*.

8. John Horgan (2000/2009), *Noel Browne – Passionate Outsider* (Dublin: Gill and Macmillan).

9. Jason O'Toole, 'One Life Less Ordinary', *Hot Press,* 23 January 2009.

10. Horgan (2000/2009).

11. 'Plan for North Central Dublin submitted', *The Irish Times,* 18 November 1976.

12. Ivor Browne (2008), *Music and Madness* (Cork: Atrium) p175.

13. Tony Gregory, 'Local Issues: Summer Project – a short history'.

14. 'Dublin's inner city residents demand re-housing in area', *The Irish Times,* 20 September-ber 1978.

15. A point mentioned by John Farrelly in interview with author.

16. Fergus McCabe, interview in 'Candida' column, *The Irish Times,* 3 March 1980.

17. Friedrich Engels (1845), *The Condition of the Working Class in England* (Oxford University Press) 1993 version, edited by David McLellan.

18. Maria Luddy (2007), *Prostitution and Irish Society 1800–1940* (Cambridge: Cambridge University Press) p186.

19. Jacinta Prunty (1995), *Dublin Slums, 1800-1925* (Dublin: Irish Academic Press).

20. Michael Bannon, J.G. Eustace and M. O'Neill (1981), 'Urbanisation: Problems of Growth and Decay in Dublin', *National Economic and Social Council Report No. 55,* (Dublin: Stationery Office).

21. Elgy Gillespie, 'East Wall holds its own special festival', *The Irish Times,* 9 June 1975.

22. 'Community and Responsibility', letter from Anthony Gregory, Secretary, North Central Community Council, *The Irish Times,* 21 December 1976.

23. Michael Punch (2009), 'Contested urban environments: perspectives on the place and meaning of community action in central Dublin, Ireland', *Interface: a journal for and about social movements* 1, 2, pp83-107.

24. 'Gregory's Trek', interview with Tony Gregory by Macdara Doyle, *In Dublin,* 1992.

25. Author's communication with Derek Speirs, 2 November 2010.

CHAPTER 3

1. Joe Kelly, then Area Community Officer with Dublin Corporation for the inner city, witnessed this encounter and kindly related it to me.

2. 'An Irishwoman's Diary', *The Irish Times*, 27 November 1978.

3. 'Tony Gregory: Giving a damn', *Strumpet,* Vol. 1, No. 4, July/August, 1981.

4. Tony Gregory, 'Political viewpoint – Inner City Neglect', *Hibernia*, 14 August 1980.

5. 'No questions, no judgments': The Saturday Interview, Kathy Sheridan to Fr Peter McVerry, *The Irish Times*, 20 December 2008.

6. 'Summerhill revisited', Fergus Brogan, *The Irish Times*, 19 January 1981.

7. 'Tony Gregory: Giving a damn', *Strumpet,* Vol. 1, No. 4, July/August, 1981.

8. Tony Gregory 'Political viewpoint – Inner City Neglect', *Hibernia*, 14 August 1980.

9. Ibid.

10. 24 February 1982.

CHAPTER 4

1. Colm Tóibín, 'Charlie Haughey Goes Downtown – An Interview with Mick Rafferty', *In Dublin*, No. 149, 18 March 1982, pp18–19.

2. Tony outlined these key concerns in a 'Féach' Irish language current affairs programme on RTÉ, broadcast on 26 February 1982, days after his election on 18 February.

3. Letter in possession of Noel Gregory.

4. Quoted in article by John McKenna, 'Enter a Kingmaker', in *Evening Herald* in 1987 in the days before Charlie Haughey was re-elected as Taoiseach.

5. Geraldine Kennedy, 'Tony Gregory: The Most Wanted Man in Irish Politics', *Sunday Tribune*, 7 March 1982.

6. Jill Kerby, 'Dublin will Live Again – Northside Picture Scoop', *Northside News West* p3, 16 March 1982.

7. Quote from Tony Gregory in *Hot Press* interview by Jason O'Toole, 2009.

8. Ronan Sheehan, Tony Gregory, Mick Rafferty, Fergus McCabe (1984), 'The Press and the People in Dublin Central: Ronan Sheehan talks to Tony Gregory, Mick Rafferty and Fergus McCabe', *The Crane Bag*, 8, 2, pp44-50.

9. This quote and the account of the interaction with Haughey are based on an article by Tony Gregory recollecting the dealings with Haughey published in the *Evening Herald* on 27 March 2001, 'The Time CJ was as good as his word'. Haughey was ill at the time and Tony ended the article by wishing him 'speedy recovery back to full health'.

10. Colm Tóibín, 'Charlie Haughey Goes Downtown – An Interview with Mick Rafferty', *In Dublin*, No. 149, 18 March 1982, pp18-19.

11. Ibid.

12. Nuala Fennell (2009), *Political Woman – A Memoir*, (Dublin: Currach Press).

13. 'True master in the art of political survival', *The Irish Times*, 25 August 2001.

14. It later merged with the Workers Union of Ireland founded by Jim Larkin to form SIPTU – Scientific, Industrial, Professional, Technical Union.

15. Dick Hogan, 'Gregory – Haughey talks repulsive, says Senator', *The Irish Times*, 9 March 1982.

16. Tony Gregory TD, Dáil Debates, 9 March 1982.

17. Eamon Gilmore TD, Dáil Debates, 4 February 2009.

18. Ronan Sheehan and Brendan Walsh (1988), *The Heart of the City* (Dingle: Brandon) p40.

19. Oliver Flanagan TD, Dáil Debates, 9 March 1982.

20. Gay Mitchell TD, Dáil Debates, 9 March 1982.

21. John Bruton TD, Dáil Debates, 25 March 1982.

22. Gay Mitchell TD, Dáil Debates, 31 March 1982.

23. Charles Haughey TD, Dáil Debates, 5 May 1982.

24. Liam T. Cosgrave TD, Dáil Debates, 5 May 1982.

25. Tony Gregory TD, Dáil Debates, 4 November 1982.

CHAPTER 5

1. Alfie Byrne is the Independent TD who can claim the greatest longevity politically. Interestingly, like Frank Sherwin and Tony Gregory, Alfie Byrne's political heartland was the inner city of Dublin. His father had been a docker. Alfie was a barman who went on to own the pub in which he worked in Talbot Street. He won a seat in thirteen consecutive Dáil elections, having previously also been an Irish Parliamentary Party MP (1915-1918) before independence. He served as TD in three different constituencies from 1922, the greater number of times as a TD in Dublin North East, which he served from 1937 to 1956. Alfie Byrne not only beat Tony on longevity, but also in the matter of achieving election as Lord Mayor, serving in that office for a remarkable period of nine years consecutively, 1930 to 1939, and for one further year in the 1950s.

2. John Horgan (2000/2009), *Noel Browne – Passionate Outsider* (Dublin: Gill and Macmillan) p293.

3. Ruairi Quinn (2005), *Straight Left – A Journey in Politics* (Dublin: Hodder Headline Ireland) p390.

4. Seamus Martin (2008), *Good Times and Bad – From the Coombe to the Kremlin, A Memoir* (Cork: Mercier Press) p226.

5. I am grateful to my colleague Dr Philip Curry for this account. His late father was one of the locals involved.

6. Máirín de Burca, 'Tony Gregory: independent Councillor', *Hibernia*, 25 October 1979, p9.

7. Author interview with Annette Dolan.

8. Lorna Donlon, 'A Day in the Life – Tony Gregory', *Sunday Tribune*, Inside Tribune, 21 October 1984.

9. Ibid.

CHAPTER 6

1. Interview with Christy Burke, 20 June 2010.

2. Andre Lyder (2005), *Pushers Out – The inside story of Dublin's anti-drugs movement* (Victoria, Canada; Trafford Books).

3. Michael Punch (2005), 'Problem drug use and the political economy of urban restructuring: heroin, class and governance in Dublin', *Antipode*, 37 (4) pp754-774.

4. Tony Gregory quoted in Sheehan et al (1984), p48.

5. 'Councillors seek talks on Dublin crime', *The Irish Times*, 22 October 1982.

6. Tony Gregory, 'Vermin who sell death shots – Gregory's View', *Daily News*, 12 October 1982.

7. Shane Butler (2002), *Alcohol, Drugs and Health Promotion in Modern Ireland* (Dublin: Institute of Public Administration) p139.

8. Geoffrey Dean, John Bradshaw and Paul Lavelle (1983), *Drug Misuse 1982-1983: Investigation in a North Central Dublin Area and in Galway, Sligo and Cork* (Dublin: Medico-Social Research Board).

9. Mick Rafferty, 'Eight Months a' Growin'', *IC – The Inner City Magazine*, Vol. 2, No. 10, May 1984, pp12-13.

10. Tony Gregory, 'Local Issues: Heroin – progress made by locals', *IC – The Inner City Magazine*, Vol. 2, No. 6, January 1984, p7; Tony Gregory, 'Local Issues: Community Action Gets Results', *IC – The Inner City Magazine*, Vol. 2, No. 9, April 1984, p6.

11. Bronagh Taggart, 'Parents against drugs', *Woman's Way*, 25 May 1984, pp12-14.

12. 'No terrorists in anti-drugs groups – TD', *The Irish Times*, 26 March 1984.

13. Des Ekin, 'Inner City Fighting Back – Drugs and Crime are on the Wane', *Sunday World*, 11 March 1984, pp12-13.

14. Tony Gregory TD, Dáil Debates, 26 June 1984.

15. Barry Desmond TD, Dáil Debates, 27 June 1984; 'Minister disputes drug-death figures', Peter Murtagh, *The Irish Times*, 28 June 1984.

16. 'Heroin claims eight in 10 days', Paul Murray, *The Irish Times*, 27 June 1984.

17. 'Desmond accused over drugs crisis', Eileen O'Brien, *The Irish Times*, 27 July 1984.

18. 'Dublin Corporation to evict drug-pushers', Frank Kilfeather, *The Irish Times*, 28 September 1984.

19. 'Anti-drugs group faces controversy', Pádraig Yeates, *The Irish Times*, 14 November 1984.

20. 'Gregory attacks heroin sentence', *The Irish Times*, 1 November 1984.

21. 'Dublin drugs protest march', Pádraig Yeates, *The Irish Times*, 7 March 1985.

22. Seanie Lambe and Jim Tracey, 'A Problem Solved?', *IC – The Inner City Magazine*, Vol. 3, No. 16, May 1985, pp. 16-19.

23. Barry Desmond (2000), *Finally and in Conclusion: A Political Memoir* (Dublin: New Island Books).

24. 'Councillors urge action on protection rackets', *The Irish Times*, December 1985.

25. See Shane Butler (2002) for detail of a Seanad debate on this issue.

26. Tony quoted in interview reported by Melanie Finn, 'The King of Independents!', *Dublin People West*, 24 April 2002, p8.

27. Tony Gregory TD, Dáil Debates, 25 July 1996.

28. Information in this and previous paragraph drawn from email Tony sent to journalist Paul Williams, kindly shared by Annette Dolan.

29. Tony Gregory, 'Why we need urgent action on drugs evil', *Sunday World*, 10 September 1995, p10.

30. Interview with Valerie Smith.

31. Interview with Annette Dolan.

32. Tony Gregory TD, Dáil Debates, 26 June 1984.

33. Tony Gregory, 'Dublin's unheeded heroin blight', *The Irish Times*, 8 April 1995.

34. David Norris, Seanad debate, 12 November 2008.

35. 'Battling the Drugs Menace', Editorial, *The Irish Times*, 28 September 1996.

36. 'Local Leaders are IRA Hitmen', *The Star*, 11 December 1996, pp6-7.

37. Catherine Comiskey (1998), 'Estimating the prevalence of opiate drug use in Dublin, Ireland during 1996' (Dublin: Department of Health and Children).

38. Quoted in J. P. Anderson, 'Dublin's Tree of Hope', Citizen's Free Press Ireland: Newsline http://lostchildreninthewilderness.wordpress.com/2010/10/07/dublins-tree-of-hope/.

39. Nuala Haughey, 'Summerhill shows how heroin pushers can be given the boot', *The Irish Times*, 29 August 2007.

40. 'Summerhill's Story', Editorial, *The Irish Times*, 29 August 2007.

41. Tony Gregory TD, Dáil Debates, 3 October 2007.

42. Dáil Debates, 22 February 2007.

43. Tony Gregory TD, Dáil Debates, 29 November 2007.

CHAPTER 7

1. Tony Gregory, 'Inner City Education', letter to *The Irish Times*, 17 March 1978.

2. INTO Press Release: Statement by John Carr, General Secretary Irish National Teachers' Organisation on the death of Independent TD Tony Gregory, 2 January 2009.

3. 'Fines anger street traders', Donal Byrne, *The Irish Times*, 19 July 1983.

4. Tony Gregory, 'Local Issues – the Gardaí and the Community', *IC – The Inner City Magazine*, Vol. 1, No. 2, August 1983, p4.

5. 'Council split on street trading', Frank Kilfeather, *The Irish Times*, 20 December 1983.

6. Tony Gregory, 'Local Issues – Rough Justice', *IC – The Inner City Magazine*, Vol. 1, No. 5, December 1983, p6.

7. 'Street traders battle for their livelihood', Pádraig Yeates, *The Irish Times*, 9 January 1985.

8. 'Dublin street traders to march', Pádraig Yeates, *The Irish Times*, 19 July 1985.

9. 'Street traders seek support of public', *The Irish Times*, 27 July 1985.

10. Interview with Christy Burke, 20 June 2010.

11. 'Bishop has talks in dispute over street traders', Pádraig Yeates, *The Irish Times*, 30 July 1985.

12. 'Gregory to consult legal advisers over jailing', *The Irish Times*, 27 January 1986.

13. Tony Gregory, 'Kid Gloves for Me in the "Joy"', *Sunday Press*, 9 February 1986.

14. 'Traders to seek to join Gregory in jail solidarity', *The Irish Times*, 30 January 1986.

15. Josephine Henry, 'Tony Celebrating with Smithfield Group', *Macro New – Macro Community Development Newsletter*, February/March 2009, p2 (special tribute issue for Tony Gregory).

16. Tony Gregory, 'Issues – Asbestos Waste', *IC – The Inner City Magazine*, Vol .4 No. 20 April/May 1986.

17. 'Gregory to mediate on prison fast', *The Irish Times*, 6 September 1982; 'Gregory to meet Doherty today', *The Irish Times*, 7 September 1982.

18. David Andrews (2008), *Kingstown Republican – A Memoir* (Dublin: New Island).

19. 'Supporters see motives behind Kelly release', Mary Maher, *The Irish Times*, 19 July 1984.

20. Máirtín Mac Cormaic, 'He won't condemn Provos or INLA', *Evening Herald*, 24 January 1985.

21. Geraldine Kennedy, 'Tony Gregory: The Most Wanted Man in Irish Politics, *The Sunday Tribune*, 7 March 1982.

22. Hanley and Miller (2009), p591.

23. 'Gregory's Trek', interview with Macdara Doyle, *In Dublin*, August 1992, pp20–22 and p80.

24. Bertie Ahern TD, Dáil Debates, 4 February 2009.

25. Martin Cowley and Denis Coghlan, 'Reagan was forewarned about walkout by TDs', *The Irish Times*, 5 June 1984.

26. Joint Oireachtas Committee on Foreign Affairs, 2 August 2006, Vol. 126.

27. Tony Gregory TD, Dáil Debates, 20 March 2003.

28. Tony Gregory TD, Dáil Debates, 22 June 2003.

29. Tony Gregory TD, Dáil Debates, 18 October 2007.

30. Tony Gregory TD, Dáil Debates, 4 November 2004.

31. Finian McGrath TD, Dáil Debates, 4 February 2009.

32. Interview with Annette Dolan.

33. 'Kelly bridge name opposed', *The Irish Times*, 16 October 1984.

34. 'Luke Kelly Bridge opened', *The Irish Times*, 31 May 1985.

35. Kevin Rafter (2005), *Sinn Féin 1905-2005: In the shadow of gunmen* (Dublin: Gill & Macmillan) p144.

36. 'Tony Gregory: One Life less ordinary', Jason O'Toole, *Hot Press*, 23 January 2009.

37. Kathy Sheridan, 'The Saturday Interview with Peter McVerry', *The Irish Times*, 20 December 2008.

38. Tony Gregory TD, Dáil Debates, 29 November 2007.

39. Garret FitzGerald, 'Gregory deal a precursor to destructive localism of politics', *The Irish Times*, 19 August 2000.

40. Basil Chubb (1982), *The Government and Politics of Ireland*, Second Edition (London: Longman) p156.

41. Tony Gregory, '1982 Deal with FF was not "horse-trading"', *The Irish Times*, 2 September 2000.

42. Joe Lee (1989), *Ireland 1912 – 1985: Politics and Society* (Cambridge: Cambridge University Press) p508.

43. 'True master in the art of political survival', *The Irish Times*, 25 August 2001.

44. Jason O'Toole, 'Tony Gregory: One Life less ordinary', *Hot Press*, 23 January 2009.

45. Hanley and Miller (2009), p437.

46. Diarmuid Doyle, 'The softening of the Dail's toughest nut', *Sunday Tribune*, 15 June 1997.

47. Rachel Borrill, 'Still Flying Solo – Independent TD and scourge of drug lords, Tony Gregory eyes the Mansion House', *Ireland on Sunday*, 26 July 1998, p15.

48. A point made by Charles Haughey's son Sean at a speech to mark the handover of his father's papers to Dublin City University, 3 February 2009, http://www.dcu.ie/news/2009/feb/DCUspeech.pdf accessed 6 September 2011.

49. *Evening Herald*, 2 June 1998, p13.

CHAPTER 8

1. Local activist Seanie Lambe says this was a big factor in his committing to Tony's cause.

2. 'Tony's Top Dog', *Irish Independent*, 30 January 2002.

3. Finian McGrath TD, Dáil Debates, 4 February 2009.

4. My thanks to Annette Dolan who suggested this point.

CHAPTER 9

1. Quoted in Patricia Kelleher and Mary Whelan (1992), *Dublin Communities in Action* (Dublin: CAN and Combat Poverty Agency) p29.

2. Tony Gregory TD, Dáil Debates, 14 June 2007.

3. A story related by Annette Dolan.

4. http://presscouncil.ie/decided-by-press-ombudsman/gregory-and-evening-herald-.1134.html, access 6 September 2011.

5. Tony Gregory TD, Dáil Debates, 7 May 2008.

6. http://www.drugsandalcohol.ie/12166/, accessed 6 September 2011.

7. Brian Cowen TD, Dáil Debates, 4 February 2009.

8. Minutes of Dublin City Council Meeting, 5 January 2009.

9. http://www.irishtimes.com/blogs/politics/2009/01/03/tony-gregory-and-radical-change/#more-16, accessed 6 September 2011.

10. 5 January 2009.

INDEX